THE COOKING WITH TRADER JOE'S Cookbook

DINNER'S DONE!

Deana Gunn AND Wona Miniati

The Cooking with Trader Joe's Cookbook: Dinner's Done!
by Deana Gunn and Wona Miniati
Photographs by Deana Gunn and Wona Miniati
Designed by 2M Creative
Cover art direction by Cat Manning Design

DISCLAIMER: The information in this book is not intended as medical advice nor intended to cure, treat, or diagnose any ailment or disease. The authors, publishers, and/or distributors do not assume responsibility for any adverse consequences resulting from adopting any health information described herein.

Published by Brown Bag Publishers, LLC
P.O. Box 235065
Encinitas, CA 92023
1-800-517-6861

Printed in China

Library of Congress Cataloging-in-Publication Data
Gunn, Deana & Miniati, Wona.
The Cooking with Trader Joe's Cookbook: Dinner's Done!/
by Deana Gunn & Wona Miniati: photographs by Deana Gunn & Wona Miniati.-1st ed.
Includes index.

I. Quick and easy cookery. 2. Trader Joe's (Store) I. Title.

ISBN 978-0-9799384-3-6 0-9799384-3-0

First Edition

Contents

Thank You Notes

It takes a village to put together a book, and those closest to us understand this well. We are indebted to our husbands, Cary and Doug, who cheerfully taste-test every recipe we make, even if it means having to try five variations of a recipe in one meal. They have been unwavering in their support and encouragement of each book in our series. Our children continue to be our most enthusiastic apprentices and shopping companions, always eager to lend suggestions on what ingredient combinations to try next. Thank you for being our most loyal fans and our most honest critics.

We are indebted to our parents, who have always encouraged us to do what we love and believed in us from day one.

We are grateful to our editor, Larry Gunn, who combed tirelessly through our recipes and gently urged us to produce excellence.

We praise our book designer, Mehdi Anvarian, for cheerfully meeting our every wish with a smile and going above and beyond to create a gorgeous book. We applaud Cat Manning whose cover design exudes fun, whimsy, and adventure.

We gratefully acknowledge Evalyn Carbrey, Registered Dietitian, and Eddy Kim, Nutritionist, for evaluating our recipes for nutritional data.

Our devoted recipe testers across the country are the best test kitchens we could ask for, always eager to try new recipes and delighting us with suggestions of their own.

Our fans motivate us to continue producing recipes and cookbooks. It's pure joy to hear your praises or to receive an email sharing a recipe. Your enthusiasm keeps us going.

And as always, our cookbooks would not have been possible without Trader Joe's stores. Oh, Trader Joe's, what would we do without you? Your crewmembers welcome us with a smile, give us a heads up on a favorite new product, and help make Trader Joe's the best grocery shopping experience in town. Thank you for inspiring us with products that get our creative juices flowing and make it fun to cook.

We thank you all!

About Us

We're Deana Gunn and Wona Miniati, two busy moms who found it necessary to change the way we cook to accommodate our increasingly hectic lifestyles. Once upon a time, we cooked meals from scratch, but with the demands of juggling work and kids, we realized that we had to get smarter about how we cooked. We wanted healthy, delicious homemade meals that would be ready quickly, and we weren't about to compromise that with take-out or fast food. As our recipes evolved, we realized that we were naturally incorporating clever shortcuts and time-saving ingredients from Trader Joe's. Our *Cooking with Trader Joe's* cookbook series shares what we've learned about preparing healthy, tasty meals using ingredients from our favorite grocer, Trader Joe's.

Our personal styles and preferences are reflected in these recipes. We use fresh produce whenever possible, and we love pre-cut veggies like Shredded Carrots, Diced Onions, or Peeled and Cubed Butternut Squash because they save us valuable time. There are days when we can afford the time to peel and cut our own vegetables or cook our own brown rice, yet there are other days when we wouldn't be able to feed our families if it weren't for Trader Joe's precooked frozen rice, precooked lentils, or precooked chicken.

Some of our recipes can be assembled in a few minutes, with very little cooking time. Others are casseroles or stews that need 30 minutes or more of "hands-off" cooking time, and the reason they also fit within our definition of easy meals is that they require little active prep time. Once the prep is done, pop the dish into the oven or leave it simmering on the stove while you help your child with homework, play with your dog, or just kick up your feet with a mug of tea and a book.

About This Book

If you love shopping at Trader Joe's and love good food, this book is for you. We show you how to take Trader Joe's unique products from around the world, incorporate them into delicious recipes, and make a healthy meal in minutes.

Have you wondered how a chef can bring together a gourmet meal in just minutes after you order? In the same way a chef relies on a kitchen prep crew to get vegetables chopped, meats marinated, and sauces simmered ahead of time, we use Trader Joe's as our own prep crew. Trader Joe's saves us time and money by giving us prepped ingredients, ready to use as shortcuts in our easy recipes. You'll be saying, "Dinner's done!" with a smile, pleased with how quickly you can put a nutritious, scrumptious meal on the table.

What makes this book unique?

1. **Photos for every recipe.** Yes, you heard it right; every recipe comes with a mouthwatering full-color photo. How else would you know if you'd like a recipe or what it will look like when it's done? We think it's necessary to have pictures with recipes, so we're continuing our tradition of giving you real pictures of real food. Unlike those in most other cookbooks, our food photos have not been touched up or doctored with any gimmicks. They are photos of real food, in our kitchens, exactly as we prepared them. We happily ate each dish after photographing it.

2. **One-stop shopping at Trader Joe's.** We're too busy to run around from store to store, gathering ingredients. And we know you are, too. So the recipes in this book have the added bonus of one-stop shopping. Get everything you need at Trader Joe's and then get ready for the easiest cooking you can imagine. Throughout the recipes, we capitalize the names of unique Trader Joe's products, such as Fresh Bruschetta Sauce or Chunky Salsa. Of course, it's not a *requirement* to get everything at Trader Joe's, but it's a convenience we invite you to embrace. And yes, we recognize that occasionally an item will be out of stock or (heaven forbid!) discontinued. We offer substitution suggestions within each recipe in case that happens, and we also keep a running list of substitutions on our website, www.cookingwithtraderjoes.com.

3. **Nutritional information.** You asked for it, and we listened. A certified dietitian and a nutritionist have evaluated each recipe, and nutritional data is given so that you can match menus to your dietary needs. We note recipes that can be made vegetarian or no-gluten, using simple substitutions.

About Trader Joe's

We are always surprised when we run into someone who's never shopped at Trader Joe's, because we can't imagine life without it! Ask someone what they love most about Trader Joe's, and you'll likely hear some of these reasons:

- ❀ **Value and quality.** At Trader Joe's, you'll find everything from the very basics to high-end gourmet food at affordable prices. All the food is high quality and delicious, with organic and natural food options found throughout the store.

- ❀ **Unique products.** Trader Joe's scouts the world for new and inspiring foods and beverages. Only the ones that pass Trader Joe's employee taste tests make it to stores.

- ❀ **Just food, no preservatives.** When you compare the labels on Trader Joe's products to items found at other stores, you'll notice something missing: a long list of chemicals, fillers, and preservatives.

- ❀ **No artificial flavors and no artificial colors.** Whether it's the "pink" in pink lemonade or the colorful candy coating on the Chocolate Sunflower Seed Drops, the colorings are natural (usually vegetable extracts) rather than synthetic food dyes. Flavorings are also natural, which not only taste better but are healthier.

- ❀ **Nothing genetically engineered.** Trader Joe's was among the first national grocers to remove genetically modified food from its private label products.

- ❀ **Actively "green."** Trader Joe's has made all kinds of environmental "green lists" for its commitment to responsible sourcing of food. Trader Joe's brand eggs are cage-free. Hormone-free dairy products are the norm. Tuna is from "dolphin-safe" water (and as a result, low in mercury).

- ❀ **Wine and beer.** In addition to great foods, Trader Joe's brings a wide and ever-evolving assortment of value-priced wines from all over the globe, including the famously nicknamed "Two-Buck Chuck" brand. Trader Joe's international beer selection is second to none.

- ❀ **Fun-filled shopping experience.** Balloons, hand-written chalkboard signs, lively music, and cheerful crewmembers decked in Hawaiian flair create a friendly and casual atmosphere.

So head on down to your nearest Trader Joe's with this cookbook in hand, and let us show you why this is our favorite grocer and our favorite way to cook.

A Word About Our Recipes

The ingredients in our recipes can be found at Trader Joe's, making the most of one-stop-shopping and time-saving shortcuts. The recipes are quick and easy, with prep times typically between 5 and 20 minutes.

Timing. The recipes in this cookbook fall into two general categories: 1) dishes that are ready to eat very quickly and 2) dishes that are assembled quickly and then spend a bit longer simmering on the stove or baking in the oven. In those recipes, we indicate "hands-off cooking time" – time you can spend doing other things while dinner cooks without you.

Healthy eating. We recognize that "healthy" is difficult to define, because it means different things to different people. To us, eating healthy means eating a balanced variety of foods, especially vegetables and whole grains. We stay away from artificial sweeteners and artificial ingredients; fortunately that's easy with Trader Joe's products. We use foods with "good" fats like avocado, olive oil, or nuts. Not all fats are created equal, so we believe it's more meaningful to pay attention to the *kind* of fat rather than adhering to fat numbers. And finally, one of the most important factors in eating well is portion control. If you eat in moderation, there is very little that is completely off-limits.

Nutritional data. We don't believe in living strictly by the numbers, but we know that some people need to regulate their diets using specific standards. So whether you follow popular diets (counting carbs, calories, or fat) or have your own regimen, we hope that the nutritional data provided in this book will guide your selection as you create healthy menus. Weight Watchers POINTS® for recipes in this cookbook are available at our website, www.cookingwithtraderjoes.com. Nutritional analysis for recipes assumes 1% milk, low-fat yogurt, and low sodium broth unless noted otherwise, and it does not include optional ingredients. When a second choice or substitution is offered for an ingredient, the first one is used for analysis.

Recommended Daily Intake:

The % Daily Values you see on labels are based on these recommended amounts, standardized for persons consuming a 2,000-calorie diet.

Calories	*2,000*
Total fat	*65 g*
Saturated fat	*20 g*
Protein	*50 g*
Carbs	*300 g*
Fiber	*25 g*
Sodium	*2,300 mg*

Serving sizes. When indicating serving sizes, we followed FDA guidelines and the recommendations of our dietitian and nutritionist. However, in practice, serving sizes can vary widely. For example, our husbands typically eat larger amounts than we do, so serving size is not a one-size-fits-all measure. If you're feeding hungry teenagers or throwing a party for the football team, allow for larger serving sizes.

No-Gluten recipes. Recipes that are no-gluten or can easily be made no-gluten are marked with Ⓖ. Please note that products at Trader Joe's may be labeled "no gluten ingredients used" as opposed to the stricter term, "gluten-free." Even if a product does not contain gluten ingredients, there is a chance of cross-contamination if it is produced in a facility that handles gluten products. Persons with celiac disease or severe gluten allergies should note that unless a product is labeled and tested gluten-free and produced in a dedicated facility, there is possibility of cross-contamination. An index of no-gluten recipes is on page 263.

Vegetarian recipes. Recipes that are vegetarian or can easily be made vegetarian are marked with Ⓥ. An index of vegetarian recipes is on page 264.

Kitchen Staples

Stock your kitchen with strategic basics, and you will have the foundation to create meals quickly. Below are some favorite Trader Joe's staples to keep on hand.

Pantry

- Extra virgin olive oil
- Balsamic or your favorite vinegar
- Vegetable, chicken, or beef broth (available in 32-oz cartons)
- Salsa
- Soyaki (teriyaki sauce) or soy sauce
- Olives, marinated artichokes, or roasted red peppers
- Pasta, rice, or couscous
- Sun dried tomatoes
- Canned beans
- Canned tomatoes
- Bruschetta, tapenade, or chutney
- Peanut butter, almond butter, or other nut butter
- Nuts (these can be stored in the freezer if they are not used quickly)
- Dressing

Freezer

- Frozen Brown Rice or Jasmine Rice (packaged as 2-cup pouches in a box)
- Frozen Pie Crust
- Frozen Crushed Garlic (packaged as frozen cubes)
- Frozen mango, berries, or other frozen fruit
- Frozen vegetables such as broccoli, peas, spinach, and green beans
- Chicken, beef, fish, shrimp, or scallops. Chicken, salmon, and steaks are often sold in separately packaged freezer-safe bags, or you can separate them into individual portions before freezing.
- Frozen boxed appetizer for unexpected guests
- Frozen French toast or waffles for those rushed mornings
- Pita bread, bagels, English muffins or other breads
- Pre-made meals such as frozen risotto or Mandarin Orange Chicken (great with Frozen Brown Rice)

Spice Cabinet

- Basil
- Oregano
- Rosemary
- Cumin
- Cinnamon
- Curry powder
- Vanilla extract
- Nutmeg
- Salt and pepper (available with convenient built-in grinders)
- 21 Seasoning Salute, an all-purpose sodium-free blend of herbs and spices

Tips For Making Mealtime Less Hectic

We know firsthand how stressful it is to open a refrigerator at 6 PM, with hungry and overtired kids (or adults!) at the table, wondering what's for dinner. May this never happen to you again! Here are a few simple rules for avoiding the dinnertime craze:

1. **Shop in advance.** Make a grocery list for the recipes you plan to make and shop ahead for the week. Use our website www.cookingwithtraderjoes.com to print out handy grocery lists for our recipes. A well-stocked fridge and pantry are your best friends when you need a dinner solution fast. If you shop with specific recipes in mind, you will also avoid wasting items bought on impulse; this especially applies to produce and meats that can go bad before you think of a way to use them.

2. **Use prepped ingredients and shortcuts.** This concept is our core strategy. Take advantage of bagged salads, cut and peeled vegetables, prepared sauces and curries, prepared dough, marinated meats, frozen brown rice, and ready-made ingredients like hummus, guacamole, pesto, and bruschetta. Shortcuts like these can cut your prep time into a fraction of what it would be if you made everything from scratch.

3. **Plan menus in advance.** Keep a calendar on the fridge noting recipes you plan to make each day. Not only will it keep you organized, it allows other family members to pitch in and get dinner started in your absence. Our recipes are simple enough for the most novice cooks, so go ahead and assign your spouse a recipe page in this book. In fact, one happy reader told us that our cookbook transformed her husband of 13 years into an aspiring chef – and he'd never cooked for her before!

4. **Include kids in the kitchen.** Even the youngest of children can work on simple tasks such as stirring or pouring. If having them help in the actual prep is not possible, have them mimic your actions using plastic bowls and make-believe ingredients. Involving kids in cooking is one of the best ways to raise healthy and adventurous eaters, instilling pride in their dishes and curiosity about what their creations taste like.

5. **Streamline your kitchen and workspace.** Most kitchen spaces are overstuffed with unused tools and duplicate gadgets. Clear out cluttered drawers, cabinets, and countertops, keeping only the tools and gadgets you use regularly.

Conversions

Volume Measurements:

3 teaspoons = 1 tablespoon
4 tablespoons = ¼ cup
16 tablespoons = 1 cup
2 cups = 1 pint
2 pints = 1 quart
4 quarts = 1 gallon
2 tablespoons = 1 fluid ounce
1 cup = 8 fluid ounces

Weight Measurements:

16 ounces = 1 pound

Abbreviations:

tsp = teaspoon
Tbsp = tablespoon
oz = ounce
lb = pound
pkg = package

Eyeballing Measurements:

Most recipes don't require painstaking measurement unless you're baking. Ingredients can usually be eyeballed.

An easy way to eyeball cup measurements is to think of the volume of an average apple. That's about a cup. Half an apple is about ½ cup. The volume of an egg is about ⅓ cup.

Pour a tablespoon of olive oil in your pan and see what it looks like in the pan. Once you get a feel for what it looks like, just eyeball it from then on.

Pour a teaspoon of salt in the palm of your hand. After you see that a few times, trust your eye as the judge.

14

Appealing Appetizers

Just Peachy Dip

Enjoy this simple mix-and-serve dip at your next party. Whipped cream cheese and spicy peach salsa are transformed into a creamy dip – perfect with pita chips, tortilla chips, or veggies. This salsa is mild; for a little more kick, choose a spicier salsa.

½ cup Spicy Smoky Peach Salsa
4 oz light whipped cream cheese

1. Mix salsa and cream cheese in a small bowl until smooth.

Prep time: *5 minutes*

Serves *8*

NUTRITION SNAPSHOT
Per serving: 36 calories, 2 g fat, 1 g saturated fat, 1 g protein, 3 g carbs, 0 g fiber, 111 mg sodium

Cheese & Chutney Mini-Rolls

We commend the British for coming up with the great pairing of cheddar and chutney. In fact, any hard or semi-hard cheese would be superb, such as Parmesan, Gruyere, or Stilton. These rolls can be made ahead of time and kept covered in the fridge. If miniature buns are not available, make tea sandwiches using multigrain bread.

1 (7-oz) pkg Mini Hamburger Buns (8 buns)

4 oz aged sharp cheddar or Cave Aged Gruyere, sliced into 8 pieces

4 Tbsp Mango Ginger Chutney

1. Make each sandwich with a slice of cheese and spoonful of chutney.

Prep time: *5 minutes*

Serves *8 (1 roll per serving)*

NUTRITION SNAPSHOT
Per serving (1 roll): 151 calories, 6 g fat, 3 g saturated fat, 5 g protein, 19 g carbs, 1 g fiber, 107 mg sodium

(GF) *Substitute brown rice bread for the buns and make tea sandwiches, or serve cheese and chutney on Savory Thins rice crackers.*

(V) ✓

Pigs-in-a-Duvet

No cocktail hour is complete without pigs-in-a-blanket. Our upscale and healthier version of this popular hors d'oeuvres is made with prosciutto and asparagus. Keep assembled rolls covered in fridge and pop them in the oven just before guests arrive.

1 (8-oz) tube refrigerated crescent rolls
8 asparagus spears, trimmed and cut in half
1 (4-oz) pkg prosciutto or 8 pieces prosciutto, cut in half

1. Preheat oven to 350° F.
2. Separate crescent dough into 8 pieces along dotted lines. Cut each triangle in half to form long, narrow triangles of dough.
3. Wrap each piece of prosciutto around asparagus. Wrap each bundle with dough, rolling from widest end to the triangular tip. Place onto baking sheet that is lightly oiled or lined (Silpat baking mats work well).
4. Bake for 15 minutes, or until golden brown.

Prep time: *15 minutes*
Hands-off cooking time: *15 minutes*
Serves *8 (2 rolls per serving)*

NUTRITION SNAPSHOT
Per serving (2 rolls): 158 calories, 10 g fat, 5 g saturated fat, 7 g protein, 12 g carbs, 0 g fiber, 580 mg sodium

(V) *Use slices of cheese instead of prosciutto.*

Stuffed Baguette Bites

Ready-made pizza dough isn't just for pizzas. Make stuffed bread with your favorite fillings, using anything from tapenade or bruschetta to meats and cheese. Think of this stuffed bread as a long calzone. Oilier fillings may split the bread along the seam, but this only makes it look a little more rustic when you serve it.

1 (1-lb) bag refrigerated plain pizza dough
¼ cup refrigerated Genova Pesto, excess oil drained
¼ cup Julienne Sliced Sun Dried Tomatoes, excess oil drained
¼ cup shredded mozzarella cheese

1. Preheat oven to 425° F.

2. On a floured surface, stretch or roll out dough to 6 x 15 inches. Spread pesto down the center lengthwise, avoiding the last inch at each end. Place tomatoes and cheese down the center.

3. Pull up sides of bread and firmly pinch a seam down the center, sealing in fillings.

4. Place dough on a lightly oiled pan or on pizza stone in oven. Bake 30 minutes, until crust is golden brown.

5. Cut into ½-inch pieces and serve warm.

Prep time: *5-10 minutes*
Hands-off cooking time: *30 minutes*
Serves *12 (2 pieces per serving)*

NUTRITION SNAPSHOT   (V) ✓
Per serving: 126 calories, 5 g fat, 1 g saturated fat,
3 g protein, 18 g carbs, 1 g fiber, 321 mg sodium

Cranberry Goat Cheese Bites

This appetizer is the kind that every host loves. No preparation – just place the ingredients on a platter or cheese board, and let your guests assemble their own servings. You get all the credit and have secretly enlisted your guests to do all the work! This holiday appetizer is a twist on our long-time favorite Goat Cheese Bruschetta Bites (*Cooking with All Things Trader Joe's,* p. 38). Cranberry Apple Butter is sweet and tangy, perfect for combining with creamy goat cheese on crackers.

1 (3.5-oz) log goat cheese
⅓ cup Cranberry Apple Butter, available seasonally
1 (4.4-oz) box water crackers (we like Multigrain & Flaxseed, but plain is fine too)

1. To make it easy to spread, let goat cheese rest for 10-15 minutes to soften.
2. Spread each cracker with goat cheese, and top with cranberry apple butter.

Prep time: *5 minutes*

Serves *8 (4 crackers per serving)*

Substitutions: *Try Pumpkin Butter instead of Cranberry Apple Butter. Or experiment with various chutneys throughout the year when pumpkin butter and cranberry apple butter are in hibernation. Whipped cream cheese can substitute for goat cheese.*

NUTRITION SNAPSHOT
Per serving: 104 calories, 2 g fat, 0 g saturated fat, 2 g protein, 20 g carbs, 1 g fiber, 40 mg sodium

 Substitute crackers with Savory Thins rice crackers.

Ⓥ ✓

Hello Portobello!

Portobello mushrooms are a favorite because they're earthy and "meaty," reasons that make them popular in many vegetarian dishes. Here, we top each mouthwatering cap with cheese, tangy sun dried tomatoes, and delicate microgreens, all served on a bed of mixed salad.

2 portobello caps, stems removed
Pinch salt
2 slices Havarti cheese
1 Tbsp Julienne Sliced Sun Dried Tomatoes, drained, and 1 Tbsp oil from jar
1 tsp finely chopped fresh basil, or 1 cube Frozen Basil
1 (5-oz) bag Organic Baby Spring Mix, or 3 cups of other salad mix
½ cup Organic Microgreens

1. Preheat oven to 400° F.
2. Place portobello caps gill-side up on a lightly oiled baking sheet. Sprinkle each with salt.
3. Bake for 10 minutes. During the last 2 minutes, add cheese on top and sprinkle on sun dried tomatoes. Remove from oven. Don't worry if portobellos don't seem quite done. They will continue to cook and will become very juicy in minutes.
4. Place a big handful of salad mix on each plate and place one portobello cap on top. Top each cap with microgreens.
5. Mix together oil and basil and drizzle on top of each cap and salad.

Prep time: *5 minutes*

Hands-off cooking time: *10 minutes*

Serves *2*

Variation: *To turn this appetizer into a heartier vegetarian meal, top with a heated veggie burger such as Trader Joe's Vegetable Masala Burgers. You can even wrap in lavash or a tortilla.*

NUTRITION SNAPSHOT
*Per serving: 227 calories, 10 g fat, 7 g saturated fat,
11 g protein, 10 g carbs, 4 g fiber, 268 mg sodium*

(GF) ✓   (V) ✓

Crab on Cucumber Boats

Roll out the red carpet for your guests and treat them to these gourmet crab bites. Skip the mayo and dress the crab simply in lime juice and herbs. Fresh crabmeat, if you can find it, is superior. If using canned crabmeat, use the refrigerated variety; the shelf-stable version won't taste fresh enough for this dish.

1 lb refrigerated lump crabmeat
1 English or hothouse cucumber
3 Tbsp fresh lime juice
2 Tbsp chopped fresh dill
2 Tbsp chopped fresh chives or green onions
Salt and black pepper

1. Slice cucumber diagonally into 24 slices.
2. Mix crabmeat, lime juice, dill, and chives. Add salt and pepper to taste, and stir to combine. If preparing ahead of time, cover and refrigerate crabmeat separately until ready to serve.
3. Place a rounded spoonful of crab mixture onto each cucumber boat.

Prep time: *10 minutes*
Serves *8 (3 boats per serving)*

NUTRITION SNAPSHOT
Per serving: 57 calories, 1 g fat, 0 g saturated fat, 11 g protein, 2 g carbs, 0 g fiber, 168 mg sodium

(GF) ✓

BBQ Pork Mini Sandwiches

Miniature barbecue pork buns are a fun, one-handed snack on game day or at your next party. Saucy shredded barbecue pork is topped with crunchy sesame-soy slaw, a great combination made even better by miniature hamburger buns. Melt-in-your-mouth barbecue pork is fully cooked and only needs to be heated.

1 (24-oz) pkg Fully Cooked Seasoned Pork Roast with Barbecue Sauce
2 (7-oz) pkgs Mini Hamburger Buns (16 buns total), or 6 regular hamburger buns
1 (10-oz) bag shredded green cabbage (about 4 packed cups)
¼ cup seasoned rice vinegar
¼ cup Soyaki
1 Tbsp toasted sesame oil

1. Preheat oven to 350° F.

2. Combine seasoned rice vinegar, Soyaki, and sesame oil in a large bowl. Add cabbage and toss well to coat. Allow slaw to sit at room temperature while pork is prepared.

3. Heat pork per package instructions, making sure to cover pork with the excess barbecue sauce. Remove from oven, shred, and mix in with surrounding sauce.

4. Toast buns if desired. Make sandwiches with coleslaw layered over pork.

Prep time: *15 minutes*

Hands-off cooking time: *20 minutes (to warm up pork)*

Serves *16 (1 sandwich per serving)*

Variation: *Use one package Hawaiian Style Maui Beef Boneless Short Ribs instead of pork. Cook short ribs as directed on package. Another variation is to top pork or beef with caramelized onions instead of slaw (thinly slice 1-2 onions and sauté in a pan with oil while meat is cooking).*

NUTRITION SNAPSHOT
Per serving (1 sandwich): 169 calories, 5 g fat, 2 g saturated fat, 11 g protein, 18 g carbs, 2 g fiber, 281 mg sodium

(GF) *Use iceberg lettuce leaves instead of hamburger buns, making tasty and low-carb lettuce wraps. Substitute tamari or wheat-free soy sauce for Soyaki.*

(V) *See our Cheese & Chutney Mini-Rolls recipe on page 17*

Ten-Layer Mexican Dip

It may seem complex at first glance, but this delicious layered dip comes together in minutes by combining convenience items with fresh ingredients. This recipe makes a big party batch and can be customized with your favorite ingredients. To make a heartier dish, substitute a can of chili for the refried beans. Enjoy with tortilla chips or pita chips.

1 (16-oz) can Fat Free Refried Beans, Refried Pinto Beans, or Refried Black Beans with Jalapeño

1 (8-oz) tray Avocado's Number Guacamole, or your favorite guacamole

8 oz (½ a container) light or regular sour cream

1 cup salsa, such as Double Roasted Salsa or Chunky Salsa

1 cup shredded lettuce

1 cup chopped tomatoes

⅓ cup sliced black olives, drained

2 green onions, chopped

2 Tbsp chopped fresh cilantro

1 cup Fancy Shredded Mexican Cheese Blend

1. Choose a glass dish, approximately 8 x 8-inches.

2. Spread refried beans on bottom of dish and continue layering with guacamole, sour cream, and salsa. If guacamole or sour cream is difficult to spread, add dollops over the previous layer. Sprinkle on lettuce, tomato, olives, green onions, cilantro and cheese.

Prep time: *10 minutes*

Serves *12*

Variation: *For an extra spicy kick, mix ½ tsp Taco Seasoning into sour cream.*

NUTRITION SNAPSHOT
Per serving: 136 calories, 9 g fat, 3 g saturated fat, 5 g protein, 10 g carbs, 3 g fiber, 469 mg sodium

(GF) ✓   (V) ✓

Warm Honeyed Figs with Goat Cheese

When figs are in season, enjoy the classic combination of sweet ripe figs and tangy goat cheese as an appetizer or even as dessert. Fresh figs spoil quickly, so plan on using them within a day or so.

12 medium or large fresh figs
1 tsp extra virgin olive oil
1 Tbsp honey
2 oz goat cheese

1. Cut each fig in half, from stem to end.
2. Heat olive oil in a skillet over medium heat. Place figs in skillet cut side down and sauté for 1-2 minutes until faces are hot and slightly caramelized. Remove from heat.
3. Drizzle figs with honey and gently toss to distribute honey.
4. Place figs face up on a platter. Place a few crumbles of goat cheese in the center of each fig. Goat cheese will soften slightly from the heat of the figs. Serve immediately.

Prep and cooking time: *10 minutes*
Serves 6 *(4 pieces per serving)*

Variation: *Substitute mascarpone for goat cheese. Or wrap prosciutto around the fig/cheese combination and enjoy a taste explosion!*

Note: *If using very small figs, cut off tops, slice down into tops just a little, sauté, and stuff with goat cheese.*

NUTRITION SNAPSHOT
Per serving: 146 calories, 4 g fat, 2 g saturated fat, 3 g protein, 28 g carbs, 4 g fiber, 35 mg sodium

(GF) ✓   (V) ✓

Instant Homemade Guacamole

Take advantage of ripe avocados and make guacamole in minutes. By mixing salsa into mashed avocado, you can customize guacamole without the effort of chopping and mixing. Adjust heat by varying the amount and spiciness of the salsa you use. One of our readers, Trista, suggested fresh Pico de Gallo and extra garlic as a flavorful variation. Serve guacamole with tortilla chips, with pita chips, on quesadillas and tacos, or on any sandwich.

2 ripe avocados
Juice of ½ lime
2 Tbsp Chunky Salsa, refrigerated Pico de Gallo, or other salsa
I tsp finely chopped cilantro or parsley, or 1 cube frozen Chopped Cilantro (optional)

1. In a small bowl, mash avocado. Stir in lime juice.
2. Add salsa and cilantro, stirring just until combined. Do not overmix, or guacamole will turn grayish from salsa blending into avocados.

Prep time: *5 minutes*

Serves *4*

NUTRITION SNAPSHOT
Per serving: 118 calories, 11 g fat, 1 g saturated fat, 1 g protein, 7 g carbs, 5 g fiber, 65 mg sodium

(GF) ✓   (V) ✓

Creamy Stuffed Mushroom Caps

Everyone loves stuffed mushrooms, and the creamy filling makes these bite-size morsels especially satisfying. For the filling, we combine spinach with Boursin, an herbed cheese spread (look for it boxed in white cardboard packaging). To create a side dish, use larger stuffing mushrooms or stuffing portobellos.

40 regular mushrooms or 18 stuffing mushrooms or small portobellos, cleaned and stems removed
1 (5.2-oz) container Boursin Garlic & Fine Herbs Gournay Cheese
3 cups (½ a 16-oz bag) frozen spinach, thawed
¼ cup bread crumbs

1. Preheat oven to 350° F.
2. Drain thawed spinach, squeezing out water firmly with hands. 3 cups frozen spinach should reduce to ½ cup thawed after water has been squeezed out.
3. Combine Boursin and spinach in a small bowl.
4. Stuff mushroom caps with spinach mixture.
5. Spread breadcrumbs on a plate. Take each mushroom and press, spinach side down, into bread crumbs, coating fully. Arrange caps on baking sheet or dish, stuffing side up.
6. Bake 12-15 minutes until water starts to appear under caps. Do not overcook.

Prep time: *10 minutes*

Hands-off cooking time: *15 minutes*

Serves *10 (2 mushrooms per serving)*

NUTRITION SNAPSHOT
Per serving: 104 calories, 8 g fat, 4 g saturated fat, 4 g protein, 8 g carbs, 0 g fiber, 148 mg sodium

(GF) *Substitute Just Almond Meal for bread crumbs.*

(V) ✓

Kickin' Artichoke Dip

Marcy C. from San Juan Capistrano won one of our recipe contests with this entry. Trader Joe's sells ready-made artichoke dips, but we think this one is even better and takes only a few minutes of prep work. The star of the recipe is the sweet and spicy pecan topping that contrasts beautifully with the dip. Serve with pita chips, tortilla chips, or Savory Thins rice crackers.

1 (12-oz) jar Marinated Artichoke Hearts, drained and chopped

1 cup reduced-fat or regular mayonnaise

1 cup shredded Parmesan cheese

1 (8-oz) pkg light or regular cream cheese, softened

1 (5-oz) bag Sweet & Spicy Pecans, chopped

1. Preheat oven to 350° F.

2. Mix all ingredients together except nuts.

3. Transfer mixture to a small baking dish and spread to flatten. Sprinkle chopped pecans on top.

4. Bake for 35 minutes, or until dip is heated through and edges are bubbly. Drape with foil if pecans begin to brown too much. Serve immediately.

Prep time: *10 minutes*

Hands-off cooking time: *35 minutes*

Serves *32 (2 Tbsp per serving)*

Variation: *If you can't bear to part with Trader Joe's ready-made Grilled Artichoke & Parmesan Dip, borrow the topping from this recipe for a tasty twist. Buy two containers of dip and empty into an oven safe dish. Sprinkle chopped Sweet & Spicy Pecans on top and bake per recipe.*

NUTRITION SNAPSHOT
Per serving: 89 calories, 7 g fat, 2 g saturated fat, 2 g protein, 3 g carbs, 1 g fiber, 172 mg sodium

(GF) ✓ (V) ✓

Chicken Satay with Peanut Sauce

A friend once joked that all food tastes better on a stick. He may be on to something. Grilled chicken is healthy but can get boring. Thread on skewers and - voila! Instant personality. The trick to juicy grilled chicken is to marinate the meat and grill at high temperature for just a few minutes. If you don't want to heat the grill or broiler, pan-fry the chicken. Don't overcook chicken or it will dry out. Leftovers can be de-skewered, cut into pieces, and substituted for cooked chicken in any of our recipes.

Chicken Satay

1 lb chicken tenders, or chicken breast cut into strips

½ cup light coconut milk

2 Tbsp peanut butter

1 tsp curry powder

2 cloves garlic, crushed, or 2 cubes frozen Crushed Garlic

2 tsp soy sauce

Wooden skewers, soaked in water for 15 minutes or more

Thai Peanut Sauce

½ cup light coconut milk

1 Tbsp peanut butter

2 tsp brown sugar

1 tsp soy sauce

½ tsp curry powder

1. Combine coconut milk, peanut butter, curry, garlic, and soy sauce in large glass bowl. Add chicken and toss to coat. Cover and refrigerate for at least 30 minutes and up to overnight.

2. To prepare peanut sauce, place all ingredients in a small saucepan over medium-low heat. Simmer for 5 minutes, stirring frequently. Remove from heat and cool before serving. Sauce will thicken as it cools.

3. When ready to cook chicken, preheat grill or broiler. Thread chicken strips onto skewers.

4. Grill for 2-3 minutes per side, or until done. Cooking time will vary depending on thickness of chicken.

Prep and cooking time: *20 minutes (not counting marinating time)*

Makes *8 skewers*

NUTRITION SNAPSHOT

Per skewer with 1½ tsp sauce: 168 calories, 8 g fat, 4 g saturated fat, 19 g protein, 4 g carbs, 1 g fiber, 348 mg sodium

(GF) *Substitute tamari or wheat-free soy sauce for soy sauce.*

Cinnamon-Pear Baked Brie

Baked Brie is one of the world's easiest and tastiest appetizers. Trader Joe's has a wide selection of soft and creamy Brie cheeses. During the holidays, they also have small Brie wheels in addition to their usual wedges. This recipe comes from one of our readers, Stephanie K. who noted that the lightness of the pear chunks is a terrific contract to the richness of the Brie. Try substituting fresh Asian pears when they are in season.

1 (8 or 12-oz) Brie wheel or 1 large wedge Brie
½ (25-oz) jar Pear Halves in White Grape Juice, or 2 fresh pears, peeled and cored
Scant ¼ tsp cinnamon
2 Tbsp chopped pecans or hazelnuts (optional)

1. Preheat oven to 350° F.
2. Slice off the very top rind of the Brie and discard. Place Brie inside a small oven-proof dish, cut face up.
3. Cut 3-4 pear halves into big chunks and scatter over top of Brie.
4. Sprinkle cinnamon and nuts over pears.
5. Bake in oven for 25-30 minutes, or until Brie starts to melt.
6. Serve with sliced crusty bread or crackers.

Prep time: *5 minutes*

Hands-off cooking time: *25-30 minutes*

Serves *8*

NUTRITION SNAPSHOT
Per serving (not including nuts): 116 calories, 8 g fat, 5 g saturated fat, 6 g protein, 6 g carbs, 1 g fiber, 178 mg sodium

(GF) *Serve with Savory Thins rice crackers.*

(V) ✓

Strawberry Mango Salsa

When ripe strawberries and juicy mango are in season, let them shine in a fruit salsa with just a hint of lime. A fruit salsa is a miniature version of a fruit salad – the very small dice makes it a condiment that you can pick up with chips or enjoy on other foods. Serve with cinnamon pita chips for a real flavor surprise or with regular pita chips for a more subdued palate. Don't throw away leftovers! Toss them in a blender with yogurt and ice for a terrific smoothie.

2 cups finely diced strawberries

2 cups finely diced mango

2 Tbsp fresh lime or lemon juice

¼ cup chopped mint or cilantro (optional)

1. Stir all ingredients gently in a serving bowl.

2. Allow to rest for 15 minutes for flavors to meld.

Prep time: *15 minutes*

Serves: *8*

Note: *Trader Joe's usually sells containers of peeled and cut mango, a convenient shortcut to enjoying this fruit.*

NUTRITION SNAPSHOT
Per serving: 41 calories, 0 g fat, 0 g saturated fat, 1 g protein, 11 g carbs, 2 g fiber, 1 mg sodium

(GF) ✓   (V) ✓

Wasabi Eggs

Deviled eggs just got sassy with a kick of wasabi! Kate S. sent us this recipe and says that whenever she takes this dish to a potluck, there are never any leftovers. Boil your own eggs (see our Helpful Tip on next page) or buy ready-to-eat hard boiled and peeled eggs, available at Trader Joe's.

1 dozen hard-boiled eggs

⅓ cup reduced-fat or regular mayonnaise

1½ Tbsp Wasabi Mayonnaise (more if you prefer more heat)

½ tsp 21 Seasoning Salute

2 Tbsp pickle relish (optional)

Paprika (optional)

1. Peel eggs, slice in half lengthwise, and empty yolks into a bowl.

2. Mash yolks with a fork and add remaining ingredients except paprika. Mix well.

3. Spoon egg yolk filling into egg white halves. Sprinkle lightly with paprika.

Prep time: *15 minutes*

Serves *12 (2 pieces per serving)*

NUTRITION SNAPSHOT
Per serving (not including relish): 112 calories, 9 g fat, 2 g saturated fat, 6 g protein, 1 g carbs, 0 g fiber, 125 mg sodium

(GF) ✓ (V) ✓

Did you know? *The reason some hard boiled eggs are a breeze to peel and others require a jackhammer has to do with the egg's freshness. The fresher the egg is, the harder it is to peel. Leave eggs in the fridge for 4-5 days before hard boiling them.*

Helpful Tip:
A ring of green around the yolk occurs when an egg cooks for too long or at too high a temperature. Use this fail-safe method to avoid the green ring. Place eggs in a pot and fill with water to cover by 1 inch. Place over medium-high flame and heat to boiling. Boil for 1 minute, then remove from heat and let rest, covered, for 10 minutes.

Bacon Wrapped Dates

You don't have to choose between salty and sweet. You can have both in this indulgent combination of crisp bacon and sweet chewy dates. Medjool dates are quite large, so we use half for each appetizer bite. With smaller dates, use them whole.

    1 lb bacon, sliced in half
    ½ lb (half pkg) Medjool dates, about 12
    24 toothpicks or small bamboo skewers

1. Preheat oven to 400° F.
2. Remove pits from dates and slice in half lengthwise. Wrap each date half with bacon slice, using a toothpick to secure the end.
3. Place on a broiling rack, which allows grease to drip as bacon is cooking. Bake for 25-30 minutes, flipping halfway during baking.

Prep time: *15 minutes*

Hands-off cooking time: *25-30 minutes*

Serves *12 (2 pieces per serving)*

NUTRITION SNAPSHOT
Per serving: 169 calories, 7 g fat, 2 g saturated fat, 6 g protein, 23 g carbs, 2 g fiber, 378 mg sodium

(GF) ✓

Did you know? *Studies have shown that ounce for ounce, dates have the highest anti-oxidant levels of any fruit!*

Soups & Salads

Mulligatawny

The first time most of us heard of mulligatawny was on Seinfeld's "Soup Nazi" episode, as Kramer's favorite soup. No wonder people were willing to wait in line for this fantastic soup of vegetables, sweet apples, mild curry, and creamy yogurt. We make a lightning-fast version using prepared mirepoix, a ready-made curry sauce, and all-natural applesauce. The soup is mild enough that kids will love eating it as much as they'll love saying the name.

1 (14.5-oz) container Mirepoix, or 1 cup each chopped onions, celery, and carrots

1 Tbsp olive oil

1 boneless chicken breast, diced

1 cup unsweetened applesauce

1 (15-oz) jar Masala Simmer Sauce

1 (14.5-oz) can diced tomatoes with no salt added

½ cup plain yogurt such as Plain Cream Line Yogurt

1 pouch frozen Organic Jasmine Rice, or 2 cups cooked rice

1. In a medium pot over high heat, add oil and sauté mirepoix for 4 minutes. Add chicken and brown for an additional minute.

2. Add applesauce, Masala Simmer Sauce, and tomato. Bring to a boil and simmer for 5 minutes. Meanwhile prepare frozen rice according to package instructions (3 minutes in microwave).

3. Take out ½ cup of soup and slowly stir into yogurt (this will temper the yogurt) and then add mixture back into soup, stirring well. This soup is meant to be thick, but if you'd like it thinner, add water or broth.

4. Place a scoop of rice in each bowl, add soup, and top with a little more rice.

Prep and cooking time: *15 minutes*

Makes *8 (1 cup plus ¼ cup rice) servings*

NUTRITION SNAPSHOT
Per serving: 197 calories, 7 g fat, 2 g saturated fat, 10 g protein, 25 g carbs, 3 g fiber, 247 mg sodium

 ✓

Ⓥ *Omit chicken. Stir in 1-2 cups cooked quinoa, if desired, for extra protein.*

Warm Spinach Salad

This salad combines the smokiness of bacon with the richness of avocado, the earthiness of mushrooms, and the tang of balsamic vinaigrette. Fresh baby spinach hosts the party of ingredients. Fully cooked bacon, available at Trader Joe's, avoids the usual splatter of cooking bacon. In similar salads, the dressing is often made with the leftover bacon grease, but we use heart-healthy extra virgin olive oil instead.

1 (6-oz) bag baby spinach

4 strips bacon (Fully Cooked Uncured Bacon or uncooked bacon)

1 (8-oz) container white mushrooms, sliced, or 1 (10-oz) bag Sliced White Mushrooms

1 ripe avocado, diced or sliced

For balsamic vinaigrette (or use ⅓ cup of your favorite vinaigrette)**:**

4 Tbsp extra virgin olive oil

2 Tbsp balsamic vinegar

1 tsp honey or agave nectar

1. Crisp fully-cooked bacon in pan and remove. If using uncooked bacon, cook in pan and remove bacon. Drain excess grease.

2. In the same pan, sauté mushrooms for 3-4 minutes, until mushrooms are plump and before they begin to release water. Do not overcook.

3. Whisk together vinaigrette ingredients and toss with spinach. Add warm mushrooms.

4. Crumble bacon on top, add avocado, and toss gently.

Prep and cooking time: *15 minutes*

Serves *4*

NUTRITION SNAPSHOT
Per serving: 256 calories, 22 g fat, 4 g saturated fat, 6 g protein, 10 g carbs, 5 g fiber, 217 mg sodium

GF ✓

Ⓥ *Substitute vegetarian bacon.*

Taco Soup

Taco soup combines the flavors and textures we all love about tacos into a hearty soup. One-pot meals like this are great for crowds because each person can tailor the toppings according to their own tastes, and you can serve it all buffet style. A soup is also easier to handle than tacos, especially for young kids. Offer guests any combination of toppings (suggestions listed below recipe). Tortilla chips are mandatory.

1.5 lbs boneless chicken breasts or thighs

1 Tbsp olive oil

1 medium onion, chopped, or 1½ cups refrigerated Diced Onions

1 (1.3-oz) pkg Taco Seasoning Mix

1 (28-oz) can diced tomatoes, undrained

2 (15-oz) cans black beans, drained

1 (15-oz) can corn, drained, or 1½ cups frozen corn

2 cups chicken broth (omit for a thicker stew)

Your choice of toppings - suggestions include:

Tortilla chips	Shredded cheese	Chopped green onions or red onions
Fresh cilantro	Avocado	Jalapeños or chiles
Sour cream	Chopped tomatoes	

1. In a large pot, heat olive oil over medium-high heat. Sauté onion until soft, about 5 minutes.

2. Add remaining ingredients and heat to boiling. Cover, reduce heat to low, and simmer for 1 hour.

3. Remove chicken, shred, and return to pot. Stir and heat through.

4. Serve with your choice of toppings.

Prep time: *15 minutes*

Hands-off cooking time: *1 hour*

Makes *8 (1-cup) servings*

Variation: *Slow cooker method: Place all ingredients into a crockpot and cook for 5-6 hours on low setting. Remove chicken, shred, and return to crockpot. Stir and heat through before serving.*

NUTRITION SNAPSHOT
Per serving (not including toppings): 256 calories, 22 g fat, 4 g saturated fat, 6 g protein, 10 g carbs, 5 g fiber, 217 mg sodium

(GF) *Choose gluten-free chicken broth.*

(V) *Substitute 1 package refrigerated Trader Joe's Chicken-less Strips and use vegetable broth.*

Potato and Kale Soup

This quintessential winter soup stars kale, a leafy winter vegetable. Grab fresh kale when it's in season - it's packed with nutrition and antioxidants. This recipe has a Latin spin, similar to Caldo Verde, a popular Portuguese soup. By cooking kale (or spinach) for just a few minutes, the leaves retain their vibrant green color. The bright blended greens make a pesto–like base for the soup, with larger chunks of kale and potato lending a satisfying heartiness. Sausage or chorizo chunks can be added for an extra punch of flavor and protein. Substitute spinach or Trader Joe's Southern Greens blend if kale is not available.

1 Tbsp olive oil

1 large onion, chopped, or 2 cups refrigerated Diced Onions

2 cloves garlic, crushed, or 2 cubes frozen Crushed Garlic

6 cups chicken or vegetable broth

1 lb potatoes, diced into ½-inch cubes

1 large bunch kale, chopped, or 1 (6-oz) bag baby spinach

Salt and black pepper

Smoked sausage or chorizo, cooked and chopped (optional)

1. Heat olive oil in a large pot. Add onion and sauté until soft, about 5 minutes. Add garlic and cook 1-2 minutes longer.

2. Pour in broth, potatoes, and chopped kale stems (these cook longer than the leaves). Bring mixture to boil. Cover, lower heat, and simmer for 10 minutes until potatoes are almost tender.

3. Increase heat and add remaining kale (or spinach). Cook for 5 minutes until leaves turn bright green. Do not overcook.

4. Blend half of the soup using an immersion blender or regular blender. Return soup to pot and check for seasonings, adding salt and pepper to taste. Top with sausage.

Prep time: *20 minutes*

Hands-off cooking time: *15 minutes*

Serves *8*

NUTRITION SNAPSHOT
Per serving (not including sausage): 112 calories, 2 g fat, 0 g saturated fat, 5 g protein, 20 g carbs, 4 g fiber, 298 mg sodium

(GF) *Choose gluten-free chicken broth and gluten-free sausage (most are).*

(V) *Use vegetable broth. Omit sausage or use soy chorizo.*

Zesty Potato Salad

Swap out heavy mayo-based dressings in traditional potato salads with this tangy and bright balsamic vinaigrette. Use your choice of baby potatoes or tri-color potatoes in red, gold, and purple to liven up ordinary potato salad. Fresh raw green beans are packed full of nutrients and add a nice crunchy balance to soft potatoes.

1 (28-oz) bag Red, Gold, and Purple Potatoes (called "Potato Medley") or baby potatoes

2 cups green beans, cut into ½-inch pieces

½ cup chopped fresh basil

For Dijon-balsamic vinaigrette (or use ½ cup of your favorite vinaigrette)**:**

¼ cup extra virgin olive oil

¼ cup balsamic vinegar

2 tsp Dijon or stoneground mustard

1 clove garlic, crushed, or 1 cube frozen Crushed Garlic

1. Boil potatoes in salted water until fork-tender, about 20 minutes. Drain and do not peel.

2. Cut potatoes into bite-size pieces.

3. Place warm potatoes into bowl and add raw green beans.

4. Whisk together vinaigrette ingredients. Pour over potatoes and toss until coated.

5. Add basil and give final toss to combine. Serve warm or chilled.

Prep time: *10 minutes*

Hands-off cooking time: *20 minutes*

Serves *6*

NUTRITION SNAPSHOT
Per serving: 207 calories, 9 g fat, 1 g saturated fat, 4 g protein, 29 g carbs, 4 g fiber, 33 mg sodium

ⒼⒻ ✓ Ⓥ ✓

Cool as Cucumber Soup

A chilled soup hits the spot on a summer day, especially one fragrant with fresh cucumber and mint. This soup requires nothing but a blender, so you won't spend even a minute over a hot stove. Serve with Parmesan Crisps or crusty baguette slices, or pair with a small sandwich.

1 lb Persian cucumbers (or other thin-skinned cucumber), unpeeled
1 cup plain yogurt such as Plain Cream Line Yogurt
¼ cup packed fresh mint leaves
½ tsp salt
2 tsp seasoned rice vinegar
Black pepper

1. Chop cucumbers into 1-inch pieces.
2. Add all ingredients to blender and purée until smooth.
3. Serve sprinkled with pepper. Garnish with extra yogurt and mint leaves, if desired.

Prep time: *5 minutes*

Makes *4 (¾-cup) servings*

NUTRITION SNAPSHOT
Per serving: 57 calories, 1 g fat, 1 g saturated fat, 4 g protein, 9 g carbs, 1 g fiber, 336 mg sodium

(GF) ✓ (V) ✓

Homemade Blue Cheese Dressing

We skipped all the mayonnaise and sour cream used in traditional blue cheese dressings and created one using Greek yogurt and buttermilk. The star component of this dressing is tangy blue cheese, complemented with lemon and garlic. Enjoy this dressing in our Blue Cheese Coleslaw (page 74) or over sweet and light lettuces, such as iceberg, Romaine, or butter lettuce. The dressing will keep for several days in the refrigerator in a covered container or jar.

4 oz (½ container) Crumbled Salem Blue cheese

½ cup cultured low-fat (1%) buttermilk

½ cup non-fat Greek yogurt

1 Tbsp lemon juice

1 clove garlic, crushed, or 1 cube frozen Crushed Garlic, thawed

Black pepper

Dried cranberries for garnish (optional)

1. Combine buttermilk, yogurt, lemon, and garlic. Gently stir in blue cheese and season to taste with pepper.

2. Serve dressing over butter lettuce or wedges of iceberg lettuce and garnish with cranberries.

Prep time: *5 minutes*

Makes *10 (2-Tbsp) servings*

Variation: *If using plain yogurt instead of thick Greek yogurt, use 1 cup plain yogurt and omit buttermilk or the dressing will be too runny.*

NUTRITION SNAPSHOT

Per serving (not including garnish): 52 calories, 3 g fat, 2 g saturated fat, 4 g protein, 2 g carbs, 0 g fiber, 173 mg sodium

Split Pea Soup

Split pea soup is one of those earthy, satisfying soups of winter. Trader Joe's regularly has spiral ham during the Christmas and Easter holidays as well as off-season. It's worth getting one as an excuse to make this easy recipe. We like to leave the soup chunky and textured, but for a smoother soup, simply purée it in a blender or cook in a crockpot. Split peas are not available at Trader Joe's, but readily found at any other grocer.

1 (16-oz) pkg green split peas

1 (14.5-oz) container Mirepoix, or 1 cup each chopped onions, celery, and carrots

2 Tbsp olive oil

4 cups (1 32-oz carton) chicken or vegetable broth

4 cups water

2 cloves garlic, crushed, or 2 cubes frozen Crushed Garlic

1 tsp oregano

Leftover ham bones and up to 1 cup chopped ham (optional)

½ tsp salt

½ tsp black pepper

Optional garnish - croutons, chopped ham, or parsley

1. Wash and drain peas (no need to soak).

2. In a soup pot, sauté mirepoix in oil until vegetables are soft, about 5-7 minutes. Add broth, water, peas, garlic, oregano, ham bones, ham, salt, and pepper.

3. Bring soup to a boil, then lower heat, cover, and simmer for 1 hour, or until peas are tender and soup is a green color.

4. Remove bones, tearing off any ham meat to add back to the soup. Taste and add more salt if needed.

5. Soup will thicken as it stands. If you prefer a thicker soup, let stand for 15 minutes, and then reheat. Ladle into bowls and garnish with croutons, chopped ham, or chopped parsley.

Prep time: *15 minutes*

Hands-off cooking time: *1 hour*

Makes *8 (1-cup) servings*

Variation: *Use 1 tsp chopped fresh rosemary instead of oregano.*

NUTRITION SNAPSHOT
Per serving (not including ham or garnish): 248 calories, 4 g fat, 1 g saturated fat, 15 g protein, 39 g carbs, 16 g fiber, 207 mg sodium

(GF) *Choose gluten-free chicken broth.*
(V) *Leave out ham bones and use vegetable broth.*

Miso Noodle Soup

A big bowl of steaming Japanese noodle soup is guaranteed to warm body and soul. Instant Miso Soup is the soup base here, and fresh shiitake mushrooms turn up the intensity of the umami-rich flavor. Use udon or soba noodles if you have them, but plain spaghetti works nicely and is easily available.

8 oz (½ pkg) spaghetti, udon, or soba noodles

2 packets Instant Miso Soup

2 cloves garlic, crushed, or 2 cubes frozen Crushed Garlic

1 cup Shredded Carrots

1 (3.5-oz) pkg fresh shiitake mushrooms, sliced, or 1 (0.88 oz) bag Mixed Wild Mushroom Medley, hydrated per instructions

1-2 green onions, sliced lengthwise into strips or chopped.

1. Boil noodles according to package instructions, omitting salt in the boiling water (the miso soup is already seasoned). Drain, rinse and set aside.

2. Meanwhile, in a medium saucepan, empty contents of miso soup packets into 4 cups water. Add garlic and bring to a simmer.

3. Add carrots and mushrooms. Simmer for a few minutes until mushrooms look tender and cooked.

4. Divide noodles between bowls, ladle soup over noodles, and top with green onions. Serve immediately.

Prep and cooking time: *15 minutes*

Serves *4*

Note: *Traditional miso soup is not vegetarian. Miso soup ingredients include dashi which is a stock made with fish.*

NUTRITION SNAPSHOT
Per serving: 276 calories, 2 g fat, 0 g saturated fat, 10 g protein, 53 g carbs, 5 g fiber, 821 mg sodium

(GF) *Substitute brown rice spagetti.*

Endive, Beet, and Avocado Salad

Crunchy endive, colorful beets, and ripe avocado chunks are married with a light citrus vinaigrette. The sweetness of the beets and creaminess of the avocado perfectly balance the slightly bitter taste of endive. Ready-to-eat boiled and peeled baby beets take the work out of this fantastic salad.

1 pkg Red and White Belgian Endive (3 small heads endive), sliced

1 (8-oz) pkg Steamed and Peeled Baby Beets, chopped into ½-inch pieces

1 ripe avocado, cubed

¼ cup Crumbled Goat Cheese

For citrus dressing:

2 Tbsp extra virgin olive oil

2 Tbsp orange juice

1 tsp fresh thyme

1. Whisk together dressing ingredients. Toss endive with dressing until well coated.

2. Add beets and avocado and give a gentle toss. Sprinkle goat cheese on top.

Prep Time: *10 minutes*

Serves *4*

NUTRITION SNAPSHOT
Per serving: 265 calories, 17 g fat, 5 g saturated fat, 10 g protein, 23 g carbs, 15 g fiber, 203 mg sodium

(GF) ✓ (V) ✓

Ginger Coconut Soup with Greens

This light soup gets it creamy base from coconut milk flavored with garlic and ginger. Healthy greens and tasty squash add color and nutrition. Trader Joe's Southern Greens are a washed and chopped blend of mustard, turnip, collard, and spinach, but you can use any combination of leafy greens in this soup. Deana's kids always ask for seconds.

1 medium onion, thinly sliced

1 Tbsp olive or vegetable oil

4 cups (1 32-oz carton) chicken or vegetable broth

1 (14-oz) can light coconut milk (2 cups)

5 loosely packed cups Southern Greens or any combination of leafy greens

1 (12 to 16-oz) bag cubed butternut squash, sweet potato, or Harvest Blend

1 clove garlic, crushed, or 1 cube frozen Crushed Garlic

1 Tbsp grated fresh ginger

Pinch salt

1. In a medium pot over high heat, sauté onion in oil until soft, about 5 minutes.

2. Being careful to avoid splattering, add broth, coconut milk, greens, squash, garlic, ginger, and salt. The greens will seem voluminous at first but cook down quickly.

3. Bring to boil, then cover, reduce heat, and simmer for 10 minutes, or until squash is tender.

Prep and cooking time: *20 minutes*

Makes *8 (1-cup) servings*

NUTRITION SNAPSHOT
Per serving: 113 calories, 6 g fat, 3 g saturated fat, 4 g protein, 14 g carbs, 2 g fiber, 78 mg sodium

(GF) *Choose gluten-free chicken broth.*

(V) *Use vegetable broth.*

Blue Cheese Coleslaw

A summer spread is not complete without the crunch of fresh coleslaw. No chopping required here – just open the bags of shredded cabbage and carrots for the quickest coleslaw in town. Blue cheese dressing adds another layer of flavors, but you can substitute ranch or other creamy dressing for a more traditional coleslaw.

1 (10-oz) bag Shredded Cabbage, or 4 cups shredded cabbage

2 cups (half a 10-oz bag) Shredded Carrots

1 batch of our Homemade Blue Cheese Dressing on (page 65) or 1 cup of your favorite blue cheese dressing

1. Toss all ingredients together until dressing is evenly distributed.

2. Chill and serve cold.

Prep time: *5 minutes*

Serves *6*

NUTRITION SNAPSHOT
Per serving: 116 calories, 5 g fat, 3 g saturated fat, 7 g protein, 10 g carbs, 2 g fiber, 316 mg sodium

(GF) ✓   (V) ✓

Winter Caprese (Beet and Mozzarella Salad)

During winter, when tomatoes aren't their best, try this twist on traditional Caprese Salad (_Cooking with All Things Trader Joe's_, p. 34), the famous Italian dish made of tomato slices, mozzarella slices, and fresh basil. Ready-cooked beets and pre-sliced mozzarella take all the work out of this dish.

1 (8-oz) pkg refrigerated Steamed and Peeled Baby Beets, sliced

8 oz Mozzarella Medallions (about ⅔ of the 12-oz pkg), or slice your own fresh mozzarella

1 Tbsp olive oil

2 tsp lemon juice or white wine vinegar

1 Tbsp fresh basil, julienned or chopped

Salt and black pepper

1. Arrange beets and mozzarella slices in alternating pattern on serving dish. Be careful with the beets – the juice will stain.

2. Whisk together olive oil and lemon juice. Pour evenly over beets and mozzarella.

3. Sprinkle basil liberally over entire dish. Sprinkle on salt and pepper to taste.

Prep time: _10 minutes_

Serves _8_

NUTRITION SNAPSHOT
Per serving: 109 calories, 8 g fat, 4 g saturated fat, 6 g protein, 3 g carbs, 1 g fiber, 122 mg sodium

(GF) ✓ (V) ✓

Watermelon Cucumber Salad

Crisp, juicy, and ultra refreshing, watermelon cucumber salad embodies summer in a bowl. It's a welcome side dish to any barbecue. We use Persian cucumbers, which are small, seedless, and thin-skinned, so you don't need to peel them. Yellow cherry tomatoes add happy sunny color. Experiment with other additions such as crunchy jicama, sweet orange segments, or a sprinkle of feta cheese.

3 cups cubed watermelon

3 cups cubed Persian cucumber (peel and seed if using regular cucumbers)

2 cups chopped tomatoes (optional)

3 Tbsp fresh lime juice (juice from 1-1½ limes)

Pinch salt

¼ cup chopped fresh basil, cilantro, or mint

1. Place watermelon, cucumber, and tomatoes in a large bowl. Add lime juice and salt, and toss gently to coat. Garnish with basil.

2. Let sit for 15 minutes before serving. If making ahead, store in fridge.

Prep time: *15 minutes*

Serves *8*

NUTRITION SNAPSHOT
Per serving: 26 calories, 0 g fat, 0 g saturated fat, 1 g protein, 6 g carbs, 1 g fiber, 14 mg sodium

(GF) ✓   (V) ✓

Posh Mâche Salad

Mâche (pronounced "mosh"), also known as lamb's lettuce, is a delicate, buttery-textured lettuce with small rounded leaves. Toss with a mild dressing, such as our lemon vinaigrette below, to enjoy its subtle flavors. To complete this salad, we add fresh fruits and Trader Joe's addictive sesame honey coated cashews.

1 (4-oz) bag mâche
2 kiwi, peeled and sliced
1 cup sliced strawberries
½ cup Sesame Honey Cashews

For lemon vinaigrette:
3 Tbsp extra virgin olive oil
1 Tbsp lemon juice
1 tsp honey
Pinch salt and black pepper

1. In a salad bowl, combine mache, kiwi, strawberries, and cashews.
2. Whisk the dressing ingredients until emulsified and pour over salad, giving a toss to coat.

Prep time: *10 minutes*

Serves *4*

NUTRITION SNAPSHOT
Per serving: 213 calories, 16 g fat, 2 g saturated fat, 3 g protein, 16 g carbs, 2 g fiber, 48 mg sodium

(GF) ✓ (V) ✓

Bountiful Bean Soup

Beans, packed with fiber, protein, vitamins, and trace minerals, are easily enjoyed in a flavorful and hearty soup. Trader Joe's sells a 17-bean blend, but this recipe will work for any kind or mixture of beans. 21 Seasoning Salute, an all-purpose sodium-free seasoning blend, pairs with fresh thyme to add complex but subtle flavor to the broth. Any combination of fresh herbs such as thyme, oregano, parsley, and bay leaf work well in this soup.

1 (1-lb) bag 17 Bean & Barley Mix, or 2 ½ cups mixed beans

2 Tbsp olive oil, divided

1 (14.5-oz) container Mirepoix, or 1 cup each chopped onions, celery, and carrots

8 cups (two 32-oz cartons) chicken broth

1 (14.5-oz) can diced tomatoes

1 Tbsp fresh thyme or ½ tsp dried thyme

1 tsp 21 Seasoning Salute

1 (12-oz) pkg Sun Dried Tomato Chicken Sausage or other sausage

1. Soak beans for 4 hours, up to overnight. (This is not necessary, but recommended.) Rinse and drain beans.

2. Heat 1 Tbsp olive oil in a large pot over medium-high heat. Add mirepoix and sauté until onions are soft, about 5 minutes.

3. Add broth, beans, tomatoes, and thyme. Bring to a boil, reduce heat, and simmer covered for 40 minutes, skimming the top if necessary.

4. Slice sausage into ½-inch pieces and sauté in 1 Tbsp olive oil over high heat for 1-2 minutes until pieces are slightly browned.

5. Add sausage to the pot and simmer for an additional 20 minutes.

Prep time: *15 minutes*

Hands-off cooking time: *60 minutes*

Makes *15 (1-cup) servings*

Variation: *Use fire-roasted tomatoes for smoky flavor, or use diced tomatoes & green chilies for more heat.*

NUTRITION SNAPSHOT
Per serving: 213 calories, 7 g fat, 2 g saturated fat, 12 g protein, 27 g carbs, 8 g fiber, 507 mg sodium

(GF) *Use dried bean mix (no barley) and select gluten-free chicken broth.*

(V) *Omit sausage or use vegetarian sausage. Substitute vegetable broth.*

Wasabi Tofu Salad

Tofu isn't boring when it's penetrated with intense flavors of soy, garlic, ginger, and sesame oil. Contrast the marinated tofu with the fresh crunch of vegetables and crisp lettuce. Swap lettuce with shredded cabbage for a salad that can last an extra day in the fridge. Addictive wasabi peas add crunch, spice, and an eye-watering wasabi kick!

1 (19-oz) pkg regular or firm tofu

⅓ cup Soyaki or Sesame Soy Ginger Vinaigrette

2 tsp toasted sesame oil

1 Tbsp apple cider vinegar

1 (5-oz) bag Baby Spring Mix, or equivalent amount of any salad greens

3 Persian cucumbers

2 green onions

1 box (pint) cherry tomatoes

½ cup Wasabi Peas

1. Dice tofu into ½-inch pieces. Place in a small bowl.

2. For the dressing, mix together Soyaki, sesame oil, and vinegar.

3. Drain excess liquid from diced tofu, then pour dressing over tofu and let marinate for 10 minutes while you prepare remaining ingredients.

4. Chop cucumbers (no need to peel) and slice green onions. Place lettuce, cucumbers, green onions, and tomatoes in a large bowl.

5. Pour tofu and dressing over salad. Toss gently to combine. When serving, top with a sprinkle of wasabi peas for added punch.

Prep time: *15 minutes*

Serves *4*

NUTRITION SNAPSHOT
Per serving: 250 calories, 12 g fat, 1 g saturated fat, 15 g protein, 23 g carbs, 4 g fiber, 692 mg sodium

(GF) *Substitute tamari or wheat-free soy sauce for the Soyaki and substitute cashews for the wasabi peas.*

(V) ✓

Garden Gazpacho

Gazpacho is a tomato-based, raw vegetable soup invented in Spain. Because it is served cold, it is most popular during hot summer months. There's only one rule about making gazpacho, and that is to keep the veggies chunky. You want a soup that's gloriously thick, not runny, with big flecks of vegetables throughout. This recipe was purposely kept mild, but you can add jalapeños or serve with a bottle of Tabasco on the side for a spicy kick. For nearly instant gazpacho, try our Pesto Gazpacho and Notcho Ordinary Gazpacho (_Cooking with All Things Trader Joe's,_ p. 82-83).

4 cups tomato juice or vegetable juice, such as Trader Joe's Garden Patch (half a 64-oz bottle)

4 Roma tomatoes, or substitute 1 (14.5-oz) can diced tomatoes

1 large bell pepper, either green or red

1 large cucumber, or 2-3 small Persian cucumbers

Half a red onion

3 cloves garlic, crushed, or 3 cubes frozen Crushed Garlic

¼ cup red wine vinegar

⅓ cup chopped fresh basil, parsley, or cilantro

Salt and pepper to taste (start with 1 tsp salt and ½ tsp black pepper)

1. Cut vegetables into 1-inch chunks. Place vegetables into a food processor, using short pulses so that vegetables are chopped, not puréed into juice. It works best to chop and process each vegetable separately, since some vegetables purée faster than others.

2. Combine all chopped vegetables in a large bowl. Add tomato juice, garlic, vinegar, basil, salt, and pepper. Stir until soup is well combined.

3. Chill at least 4 hours and preferably overnight. The longer the soup sits, the better the flavors combine. Serve cold.

Prep time: _20 minutes_

Makes _8 (1-cup) servings_

NUTRITION SNAPSHOT
Per serving: 44 calories, 0 g fat, 0 g saturated fat, 2 g protein, 9 g carbs, 2 g fiber, 590 mg sodium

(GF) ✓ (V) ✓

Hearty Minestrone with Pesto

Minestrone is as Italian as pasta. Minestrone literally means "big soup" because it is made with a long list of vegetables, any combination that is in season. It's also common to add beans and rice or pasta, making this a hearty one-dish meal. This recipe makes a very large batch, so get those freezable containers ready! Adding green beans toward the end preserves their bright color. One bite of this fresh-tasting soup and you will never go back to canned minestrone again.

2 Tbsp olive oil

1 (4-oz) pkg Cubetti Pancetta (pancetta mini-cubes) (optional)

1 (14.5-oz) container Mirepoix, or use 1 cup each chopped onions, celery, and carrots

3 cloves garlic, crushed, or 3 cubes frozen Crushed Garlic

1 (28-oz) can diced tomatoes, do not drain

4 cups (1 32-oz carton) chicken or vegetable broth

2 cups water

2 cups shredded cabbage, Swiss chard, or spinach leaves, firmly packed

1 large boiling potato, diced

3 cups sliced zucchini, about 2 medium or 3 small

1 (15-oz) can kidney beans or cannelloni beans, drained

1 Tbsp fresh chopped oregano, or 1 tsp dried oregano

2 cups dry pasta, such as fusili, rotelle, elbows, or shells

1½ cups green beans, cut into bite-size pieces

½ cup refrigerated Genova Pesto or jarred Pesto alla Genovese

Parmesan cheese for garnish (optional)

1. Heat oil in a large soup pot over medium-high heat. Add pancetta and cook until lightly browned, about 5 minutes.

2. Add mirepoix and cook until onions are soft, about 5 minutes longer.

3. Add all remaining ingredients except pasta, green beans, pesto, and Parmesan. Bring soup to a boil, cover, reduce heat, and simmer for 30 minutes.

4. Add pasta and green beans. Cook 10 minutes longer or for time indicated on pasta package instructions.

5. Stir in pesto and garnish with Parmesan.

Prep time: *20 minutes*

Hands-off cooking time: *40 minutes*

Makes *16 (1-cup) servings*

NUTRITION SNAPSHOT
Per serving (not including garnish): 173 calories, 6 g fat, 1 g saturated fat, 6 g protein, 25 g carbs, 4 g fiber, 229 mg sodium

(GF) *Choose gluten-free chicken broth and substitute gluten-free brown rice pasta.*

(V) *Use vegetable broth.*

Breakout Broccoli Salad

Boring broccoli salad takes on a new life with zesty dressing, crunchy rosemary-infused almonds, and tart cherries. Instead of steaming the broccoli, we blanch it briefly, bringing out the vibrant green color and retaining all the crunch. To cut down the prep time, skip the blanching and use raw broccoli. You can also substitute your favorite ready-made creamy dressing for the homemade one here.

1 (12-oz) bag Organic Broccoli Florets, or 6 cups of broccoli cut into bite-size pieces
¼ cup dried Tart Montmorency Cherries or raisins
⅓ cup Marcona Almonds with Rosemary, roughly chopped or sliced almonds
Pinch salt

For dressing:
3 Tbsp mayonnaise
1 tsp red wine vinegar
1 tsp lemon juice
1 tsp sugar

1. Bring 6 cups of water to boil. Add broccoli to boiling water, wait 10 seconds, and then drain. Rinse with cold water and leave to drain and cool.
2. Whisk together dressing ingredients and toss broccoli with dressing. Add cherries, almonds, and salt, tossing again.

Prep and cooking time: *10 minutes*

Serves *4*

NUTRITION SNAPSHOT
Per serving: 224 calories, 15 g fat, 2 g saturated fat, 6 g protein, 21 g carbs, 5 g fiber, 177 mg sodium

(GF) ✓ (V) ✓

Corn Chowder

Creamy, thick, and chunky, just like a good chowder should be. This soup is heavenly in summer when fresh sweet corn is in season, but it's also a soothing winter soup with frozen corn or Trader Joe's famous canned corn. The high starch content in russet potatoes helps to thicken the soup; using other varieties of potatoes may result in watery chowder. Serve with Oyster Crackers or crusty bread.

3 ears corn, shucked, or 3 cups canned or frozen corn

1 large onion, chopped, or 2 cups refrigerated Diced Onions

2 Tbsp olive oil

¼ cup flour

2 chicken broth or vegetable broth

2 cups milk

1 large russet potato, peeled and diced (1-½ cups)

1 cup diced frozen cooked shrimp, thawed

1 tsp fresh thyme, chopped

½ tsp salt

½ tsp black pepper

Shredded cheddar cheese for garnish (optional)

Chili powder (optional)

Salt to taste

1. Heat olive oil in a soup pot over medium-high heat. Add onion and sauté until soft, about 5 minutes.

2. Add flour and cook for 1 minute. Whisk in broth and milk. Add corn and diced potato. Bring to a boil, reduce heat, and simmer for 10 minutes until potato is cooked and soup is thick.

3. Add shrimp, thyme, salt, and pepper. Heat through and serve. Garnish with cheese and chili powder.

Prep time: *15 minutes*

Hands-off cooking time: *10 minutes*

Makes *6 (1-cup) servings*

NUTRITION SNAPSHOT
Per serving (not including garnish): 243 calories, 7 g fat, 1 g saturated fat, 9 g protein, 40 g carbs, 3 g fiber, 79 mg sodium

(GF) *Choose gluten-free broth.*

(V) *Use vegetable broth and omit seafood.*

Shrimp and Avocado Salad

Remember the shrimp salad you had growing up, swimming in mayo and piled onto avocado halves? Our modern version is lighter, tastier, and more sophisticated. We use Chilean langostino tails, which taste like lobster. They don't appear often, so when they do, stock up. Shrimp is also delicious in this light salad.

1 (12-oz) bag frozen cooked Langostino Tails, thawed, or ¾ lb frozen cooked shrimp, thawed

1 large ripe avocado, cut into wedges or bite-size chunks

1 grapefruit, peeled and segmented

1 (5-oz) bag butter lettuce

¼ cup chopped pistachios

For white wine vinaigrette (or use ⅓ cup of your favorite light-flavored vinaigrette):

2 Tbsp white wine vinegar

3 Tbsp olive oil

½ clove garlic, crushed, or ½ cube frozen Crushed Garlic

¼ tsp salt

1. Arrange butter lettuce onto serving platter or individual plates.

2. Lightly toss avocado and grapefruit pieces; acid from the grapefruit will keep avocado from turning brown. Place evenly on top of lettuce.

3. Toss langostino tails with vinaigrette. Scatter evenly on salad, drizzling any remaining vinaigrette on top.

4. Sprinkle with pistachios.

Prep time: *15 minutes*

Serves: *4*

NUTRITION SNAPSHOT
Per serving: 310 calories, 20 g fat, 3 g saturated fat, 20 g protein, 13 g carbs, 4 g fiber, 275 mg sodium

(GF) ✔

Green Waldorf Salad

This famous salad was invented at the Waldorf Astoria Hotel in New York City and has since made appearances at countless holiday gatherings and buffet spreads. The original recipe calls for red apples, celery, and mayonnaise – and nothing else. We opt for tart flavors and lively green colors, while preserving the crunchiness and juiciness of the classic.

2 Granny Smith apples, diced
2 cups green grapes, halved
½ cup slivered almonds
¼ cup plain yogurt
1 Tbsp honey or agave nectar
¼ tsp salt
¼ tsp black pepper

1. Whisk yogurt, honey, salt, and pepper in a large bowl.
2. Stir in apples, grapes, and almonds. Toss lightly to coat.
3. Keep in fridge until ready to serve.

Prep time: *15 minutes*

Serves: *6*

NUTRITION SNAPSHOT
Per serving: 114 calories, 5 g fat, 0 g saturated fat, 3 g protein, 17 g carbs, 3 g fiber, 97 mg sodium

(GF) ✓   (V) ✓

- Five-Minute Shiitake Fried Rice
- White Lightning Chili
- Shrimp Lettuce Wraps
- Linguine and Clams
- Pesto Pita Pizza
- Salmon Panzanella
- Kinda-Greek Pasta Salad
- Scallops Marsala Over Capellini
- Brown Butter Cod
- Pollo y Guac Tacos
- Grilled Veggie Sandwich with Lemon Garlic Sauce
- Chicken in White Wine Sauce
- Macadamia-Crusted Mahi Mahi
- Plum Good Stew
- Yin Yang Shrimp and Grits
- Lime-Marinated Chicken Fajitas
- Roasted Red Pepper and Mozzarella Sandwich
- Spaghetti alla Carbonara
- Baked Gnocchi
- Grilled Lentil Wraps
- Speedy Chicken & Roasted Pepper Quesadillas

- Chole and Naan
- Ham & Brie Sandwich
- Arugula Pesto Pasta
- Easy Chicken Parmigiana
- No-Bean Turkey Chili
- Lentil Haystacks
- Super-quick Mushroom Faux-Risotto
- Eggplant Cutlet Sandwich
- Coq Au Vin
- Salmon Nicoise Salad
- My Big Fat Greek Quiche
- Spinach & Artichoke Dip Pizza
- Summery Shrimp Capellini
- Philly Cheese Steak
- Sloppy Joe's
- Tamale Bake
- Mediterranean Baked Fish
- Arugula Salad Pizza
- Herbed Citrus Shrimp with Quinoa and Goat Cheese
- Mom's Meatloaf

Main Meals

Five-Minute Shiitake Fried Rice

Sure, you can buy frozen fried rice, but why not make it yourself in about the same time and customize the ingredients to your taste? This fried rice gets its flavors from umami-rich shiitake mushrooms and the combination of ginger, garlic, and sesame in Trader Joe's Soyaki. It's ready in a snap with hardly any prep work, using Trader Joe's frozen Jasmine Rice.

1 pouch frozen Organic Jasmine Rice, or 2 cups cooked rice

1 tsp olive oil

5-6 shiitake mushrooms, sliced

1½ cups frozen Organic Foursome, Soycutash, or other vegetable mix

2 Tbsp Soyaki

1 Tbsp seasoned rice vinegar

1 tsp toasted sesame oil

2 green onions, chopped or cut lengthwise (as in photo)

1. Heat rice according to package instructions (3 minutes in microwave).

2. Heat oil in a pan or wok over high heat and sauté mushrooms and frozen vegetables (no need to thaw) for 2 minutes until mushrooms soften.

3. Remove pan from heat and add Soyaki, vinegar, and sesame oil, stirring mixture. Add rice and stir to combine. Serve immediately, topped with green onions.

Prep and cooking time: *5 minutes*

Serves *2 (or 4 as a side)*

Variation: *Use your own blend of vegetables, Frozen Brown Rice instead of Jasmine, regular mushrooms instead of shiitake, add tofu or pre-cooked chicken (sold as Just Chicken), or tweak seasonings to your taste. To make this dish heartier, top with a fried or poached egg. For something a little different, try our Couscous Bowl (The Trader Joe's Companion, p. 38), which takes its inspiration from fried rice but uses pearl couscous instead of rice.*

NUTRITION SNAPSHOT

Per serving: 384 calories, 8 g fat, 1 g saturated fat, 8 g protein, 71 g carbs, 6 g fiber, 392 mg sodium

(GF) *Substitute tamari or wheat-free soy sauce for Soyaki.*

(V) ✓

Helpful Tip:
Trader Joe's Just Chicken is an easy addition to any pasta salad, chicken salad, quesadilla or casserole. If you're not familiar with Just Chicken, it's just that: precooked charbroiled chicken with no preservatives or artificial additives, available in the refrigerated section.

White Lightning Chili

Hearty white chili is a tomato-less alternative to traditional chili. This sweet and spicy white chili gets its flavor and kick from Trader Joe's well known Corn and Chile Tomato-less Salsa. Quinoa is a double-duty ingredient, thickening the chili as well as adding protein, magnesium, calcium, and iron. The quinoa will absorb most of the liquid and soften, becoming a flavorful component that binds the chili together.

1 (1-lb) pkg Just Chicken (or 4 cups cooked chicken), cut or shredded into bite-size chunks

2 cups chicken or vegetable broth

½ cup quinoa, rinsed

1 (15-oz) can white kidney beans (cannelloni beans), rinsed and drained

1 (15-oz) can pinto beans, rinsed and drained

1 (13.75-oz) jar Corn and Chile Tomato-less Salsa

1 cup Shredded Three Cheese Blend for garnish (optional)

1. Pour broth into a medium or large pot. Add quinoa and bring to a boil.

2. Add remaining ingredients and return to a boil. Lower heat, cover, and simmer for 20-25 minutes, or until most of the liquid is absorbed.

3. Serve in bowls, topping with shredded cheese.

Prep time: *5 minutes*

Hands-off cooking time: *20-25 minutes*

Makes *8 (1-cup) servings*

Note: *When reheating leftovers, add extra liquid, either broth or water.*

NUTRITION SNAPSHOT
Per serving (not including cheese garnish): 284 calories, 1 g fat, 0 g saturated fat, 25 g protein, 39 g carbs, 8 g fiber, 487 mg sodium

(GF) *Choose gluten-free broth.*

(V) *Use vegetable broth and substitute two packages of Trader Joe's Chickenless Strips.*

Did you know? *Quinoa cooking instructions often recommend first rinsing the quinoa. Quinoa seeds naturally have a soapy coating that can be bitter. Processing usually removes this coating, but it varies from brand to brand, so it's a good idea to give quinoa a quick rinse before using. If the water becomes slightly sudsy, then you know that the coating was there.*

Shrimp Lettuce Wraps

Capture the flavor of restaurant lettuce wraps at home in minutes. Diced shrimp and veggies combined with the zing of an Asian-inspired sauce are wrapped in fresh iceberg lettuce leaves. This dish is best served family style, with the shrimp mixture in one bowl next to the lettuce leaves and optional toppings.

1 lb large uncooked shrimp (peeled with tail off), thawed if frozen

2 Tbsp Soyaki

1 tsp toasted sesame oil

1 clove garlic, crushed, or 1 cube frozen Crushed Garlic

1 Tbsp lemon or lime juice

2 green onions, chopped

1 Tbsp vegetable or olive oil

1 red bell pepper, diced, or 1 cup Mélange à Trois bell pepper strips, thawed

½ cup Shredded Carrots

5 shiitake mushrooms, thinly sliced

¼ tsp each salt and black pepper

1 head iceberg lettuce, leaves separated

Optional toppings:

⅓ cup peanuts or Thai Lime Chile Cashews, roughly chopped

⅓ cup fresh basil, chopped

1. In a small bowl, combine Soyaki, sesame oil, garlic, lemon juice, and green onions to create a sauce. Set aside.

2. Dice shrimp. In a wok or skillet over high heat, add vegetable oil and stir-fry shrimp for 1 minute.

3. Add bell pepper, carrots, mushrooms, salt, and pepper. Stir-fry for an additional minute, or until shrimp is opaque and firm. Do not overcook shrimp.

4. Remove pan from heat and stir in sauce. Transfer mixture to a serving bowl.

5. Serve by putting 2 Tbsp of shrimp mixture into each lettuce leaf, adding toppings, and wrapping like a mini burrito.

Prep and cooking time: *25 minutes*

Serves *4*

NUTRITION SNAPSHOT
Per serving (not including toppings): 188 calories, 7 g fat, 1 g saturated fat, 21 g protein, 14 g carbs, 3 g fiber, 160 mg sodium

(GF) *Substitute tamari or wheat-free soy sauce for Soyaki.*

(V) *Substitute equivalent amount of firm tofu or seitan cut into matchsticks.*

Linguine and Clams

Frozen Steamer Clams come ready to cook, fully seasoned in their own garlic butter sauce. Toss all the contents into a pan and voila! A gourmet seafood dinner is ready in under 10 minutes. Lemon juice and basil perk up the dish with a burst of freshness.

4 oz (¼ pkg) linguine or other pasta
1 (16-oz) box frozen Steamer Clams in Garlic Butter Sauce
Juice of 1 lemon
2 Tbsp chopped fresh basil
Shredded Parmesan cheese (optional)

1. Cook pasta in salted boiling water.

2. About 5 minutes before pasta is done, cook clams in a skillet according to package instructions. Drain pasta while clams are cooking.

3. Squeeze lemon juice onto clams. Pour clams and sauce over pasta, and sprinkle liberally with basil and Parmesan.

Prep and cooking time: *10 minutes*

Serves *2*

Variation: *Skip the pasta and serve with crusty bread as an appetizer.*

Note: *For extra creaminess, stir ¼ cup heavy cream into cooked clams in step 2.*

NUTRITION SNAPSHOT
Per serving (not including cheese garnish): 309 calories, 6 g fat, 3 g saturated fat, 18 g protein, 47 g carbs, 2 g fiber, 105 mg sodium

(GF) *Substitute brown rice pasta.*

Pesto Pita Pizza

These easy individual-size pizzas are a breeze to assemble, using pita pockets that bake up delicious and crispy on the edges. The best part is that each pizza can be customized using your own choice of toppings. Adding fresh tomato and basil after baking creates a garden-fresh contrast to the hot, crisp pizza.

2 standard-size (7-inch diameter) pita pockets
4 Tbsp refrigerated Genova Pesto or jarred Pesto alla Genovese
½ cup shredded mozzarella cheese
1 ripe tomato, diced (about ½ cup)
2 Tbsp chopped fresh basil

1. Preheat oven to 400° F.
2. Place pitas on baking sheet, lightly sprayed with cooking oil.
3. Spread 2 Tbsp pesto on each pita. Top each with ¼ cup of cheese.
4. Bake for 8 minutes, until cheese is bubbly.
5. Remove from oven and top with tomato and basil.

Prep time: *5 minutes*

Hands-off cooking time: *8 minutes*

Serves *2*

Variation: *Use marinara (or tomato sauce), black olives, and mozzarella.*

NUTRITION SNAPSHOT
Per serving: 321 calories, 17 g fat, 3 g saturated fat, 10 g protein, 31 g carbs, 2 g fiber, 388 mg sodium

Ⓥ ✓

Salmon Panzanella

Panzanella is a popular bread salad from Italy, originally a peasant food that has become fancy enough for restaurant menus and party spreads. Panzanella is made using stale, day-old, or even week-old bread. Don't try to use fresh-baked bread; it will get soggy when tossed with the vinaigrette. A baguette, ciabatta, or any hearty crusty bread works. Never throw out stale bread again!

1 lb salmon, cut into ¾-inch chunks

5 cups cubed baguette or ciabatta bread (day-old is preferred), cut into ¾-inch cubes

2 Tbsp olive oil, divided

Half a red onion, thinly sliced

2 cups chopped tomatoes or halved cherry tomatoes

2 cups sliced cucumbers (preferably Persian or hothouse)

1 bell pepper, cut into bite-size pieces

1 Tbsp capers, drained

¼ cup chopped fresh basil

½ tsp salt

¼ tsp black pepper

For Champagne vinaigrette (or use ⅓ cup of your favorite vinaigrette):

1 tsp Garlic Aioli Mustard Sauce, or ½ tsp Dijon mustard + ½ tsp crushed garlic

2 Tbsp Orange Muscat Vinegar or white wine vinegar

¼ cup olive oil

¼ tsp salt

Pinch black pepper

1. Preheat oven to 450° F.

2. Season salmon with salt and pepper. Toss with ½ Tbsp olive oil until pieces are evenly coated.

3. Toss bread cubes with 1½ Tbsp olive oil until evenly coated. Place salmon, bread, and onion on a baking sheet in a single layer (or if you prefer the bite of raw onion, reserve uncooked). Bake for 10-12 minutes, or until salmon is cooked and bread is toasted. Stir halfway through baking time to roast evenly.

4. In a large bowl, combine tomatoes, cucumbers, bell pepper, capers, and basil. Add salmon, bread, and onion.

5. Whisk together vinaigrette ingredients, add to bowl, and toss until evenly coated. Allow salad to sit for 20 minutes for croutons to soak up flavor.

Prep time: *15 minutes*

Hands-off cooking time: *10-12 minutes*

Serves *6*

NUTRITION SNAPSHOT

Per serving: 364 calories, 19 g fat, 3 g saturated fat, 21 g protein, 26 g carbs, 3 g fiber, 611 mg sodium

(GF) *Substitute brown rice bread.*

(V) *Omit salmon.*

Helpful Tip:
Store stale pieces of bread in a Ziploc bag in the freezer. Use accumulated bread to make panzanella or bread crumbs.

Helpful Tip:

When cooking brown rice or whole wheat pasta, be careful not to overcook it, else the texture will become gummy. Drain and rinse as soon as pasta is al dente. Brown rice pasta tends to stiffen and become rubbery after refrigeration, so it is best eaten the same day.

Kinda-Greek Pasta Salad

Crunchy cucumbers, tangy feta, flavor-packed sun dried tomatoes, and briny black olives come together in a Greek-inspired pasta dish that is good cold or warm. Seasoned olive oil from the jar of sun dried tomatoes coats the pasta with more complex flavor than plain olive oil. Holistic health counselor Marcy Rosenthal developed this easy recipe; it shows how easy healthy cooking can be with a well stocked pantry and convenience items.

1 (16-oz) bag whole wheat or regular penne pasta, or 2 (16-oz) bags frozen Just Pasta Penne

1 (8.5-oz) jar Julienne Sliced Sun Dried Tomatoes; do not drain oil

1 (3.8-oz) can sliced black olives, drained

1 (6-oz) container Crumbled Feta with Mediterranean Herbs

1 large cucumber or 4 Persian cucumbers, chopped (2 cups)

1 Tbsp red wine vinegar or balsamic vinegar

½ pkg (8 oz) frozen Just Grilled Chicken Strips (or grill 1 breast yourself)

1. Cook pasta according to package instructions. Rinse with cool water and drain. While pasta is cooking, prepare chicken and cut into bite-size pieces.

2. Mix all ingredients with pasta and serve.

Prep time: *10 minutes*

Hands-off cooking time: *10 minutes*

Serves *8*

NUTRITION SNAPSHOT
Per serving: 423 calories, 15 g fat, 3 g saturated fat, 22 g protein, 51 g carbs, 6 g fiber, 528 mg sodium

(GF) *Substitute brown rice pasta.*

(V) *Omit chicken or substitute Trader Joe's Chickenless Strips.*

Scallops Marsala Over Capellini

Marsala sauce dishes are traditionally made with chicken or veal, but here we choose sweet jumbo scallops for an upscale version. Butter-seared scallops fit perfectly with the mouth-watering wine and mushroom sauce. Serve over thin pasta such as vermicelli or capellini, or enjoy over Trader Joe's Garlic Mashed Potatoes.

8 frozen jumbo scallops, thawed

8 oz (½ pkg) capellini or other thin pasta

¼ tsp salt

1 tsp olive oil

1 Tbsp butter

1 medium onion, diced, or 1 cup refrigerated Diced Onions

1 (8-oz) pkg white mushrooms, sliced, or 1 (10-oz) pkg Sliced White Mushrooms

2 cloves garlic, crushed, or 2 cubes frozen Crushed Garlic

Pinch salt

¾ cup Marsala wine

½ cup half-and-half

1 tsp cornstarch

¼ cup parsley, chopped

1. Cook pasta according to package instructions. Drain and set aside.

2. Pat scallops dry using paper towels and sprinkle with salt. Heat pan over high heat and add oil and butter. When pan is hot and butter is melted, add scallops and sear 30 seconds each side. Remove and set aside (scallops will be added back in for additional cooking).

3. In the same pan over high heat, sauté onion until soft, about 5 minutes. Add mushrooms, garlic, and salt, sautéing for additional 2-3 minutes until mushrooms are cooked but plump.

4. Lower heat and add Marsala wine and half-and-half, simmering until sauce thickens. Don't worry if the wine flames. The alcohol will burn off quickly, or you can cover momentarily with a lid. Don't bring sauce to a boil or half-and-half will curdle.

5. Mix cornstarch with 1 tsp water and stir into sauce to thicken. Stir in parsley, add scallops back to pot, and simmer for additional 2 minutes.

6. Serve over pasta.

Prep and cooking time: *25 minutes*

Serves *4*

NUTRITION SNAPSHOT
Per serving: 372 calories, 9 g fat, 4 g saturated fat, 20 g protein, 56 g carbs, 3 g fiber, 471 mg sodium

(GF) *Substitute brown rice pasta.*

Helpful Tip:
To thaw frozen scallops quickly, run cold water over them. Never use warm water.

Brown Butter Cod

A lemony brown butter sauce adds rich flavor to simple white fish. Any white fish such as cod, sole, striped sea bass, or tilapia will work for this recipe. Serve over Trader Joe's Garlic Mashed Potatoes, over rice, or alongside roasted vegetables.

1 lb Alaskan Cod Fillets, thawed if frozen
½ tsp Lemon Pepper
½ tsp salt
2 Tbsp butter, divided
1 Tbsp olive oil
1 Tbsp capers
1 clove garlic, crushed, or 1 cube frozen Crushed Garlic
2 Tbsp lemon juice
1 Tbsp half-and-half
1 Tbsp chives

1. Pat fish dry using paper towels. Rub Lemon Pepper and salt on both sides of fillets.
2. Heat oil and 1 Tbsp butter in a skillet over high heat and sauté fish 2 minutes each side.
3. Transfer fish to serving dish. Remove pan from heat and add capers, garlic, lemon, half-and-half, and remaining butter. Scrape pan to loosen any brown bits and stir to create a sauce.
4. Pour sauce over each fillet.

Prep and cooking time: *15 minutes*

Serves *4*

NUTRITION SNAPSHOT
Per serving: 149 calories, 7 g fat, 4 g saturated fat, 20 g protein, 1 g carbs,
0 g fiber, 464 mg sodium

(GF) ✓

Helpful Tip:

Corn tortillas are stiff and rubbery until they are heated. An easy way to heat a large number of corn tortillas is to steam them in the microwave. First, separate tortillas from each other. Drizzle 2-3 Tbsp water on a clean kitchen towel. Fan out the tortillas slightly, wrap the towel around them, and heat in microwave for 1 ½ -2 minutes. Steamed tortillas will stay warm for 10 minutes.

Pollo y Guac Tacos

At roadside stands in Baja California, soft tacos are made with pollo asado (flame-roasted chicken), spicy guacamole, and lots of fresh cilantro. Trader Joe's Pollo Asado Autentico captures that authentic flavor and makes it easy to enjoy in minutes.

1 (1.5-lb) pkg Pollo Asado Autentico
1 (12-oz) pkg corn tortillas (12 tortillas)
1 (8-oz) tray Avocado's Number Guacamole or our Instant Homemade Guacamole recipe (page 35)
Fresh cilantro or parsley, chopped

1. Cook chicken according to package instructions. When cooked, shred into bite-size pieces.
2. Heat tortillas (see Helpful Tip).
3. In each tortilla, add guacamole, top with chicken, and garnish with cilantro.

Prep and cooking time: *10 minutes*

Serves *6 (2 tacos per serving)*

NUTRITION SNAPSHOT
Per serving: 317 calories, 9 g fat, 2 g saturated fat, 29 g protein, 28 g carbs, 5 g fiber, 308 mg sodium

(GF) ✓
(V) *Substitute Trader Joe's Chickenless Strips.*

Grilled Veggie Sandwich with Lemon Garlic Sauce

In this sandwich, rich eggplant and zucchini slices contrast with fresh, peppery arugula and tangy feta. "Misto Alla Griglia," marinated grilled eggplant and zucchini, takes all the work out of preparing the grilled veggies. The measurements are approximate – use more grilled veggies per sandwich if desired. For a picnic or party batch, see note below for making multiple sandwiches. Don't skip the lemon garlic sauce - it adds incredible flavor.

¼ (16-oz) bag frozen Misto Alla Griglia (Marinated Grilled Eggplant & Zucchini)
1 Petits Pains Rustiques (large Country Style French Rolls)
½ cup fresh arugula, loosely packed
1 Tbsp Crumbled Feta with Mediterranean Herbs

For lemon garlic sauce:

1 Tbsp mayonnaise
1 tsp lemon juice
1 cube frozen Crushed Garlic or 1 small cube, clove garlic, crushed

1. Thaw Misto alla Griglia overnight in fridge or microwave per package instructions. Use cold or heat in microwave until warm.
2. Cut roll in half.
3. In a small bowl, stir together ingredients for Lemon Garlic Sauce until smooth.
4. Build sandwich by drizzling sauce onto bottom of roll. Add arugula, eggplant and zucchini slices, and finish with a topping of feta. Cut in half and serve.

Prep time: *10 minutes*

Serves *2*

Note: *1 (16-oz) bag of Misto Alla Griglia and 1 (8-oz) bag of Petits Pains Rustiques is enough to make 4 large sandwiches (8 servings).*

NUTRITION SNAPSHOT
Per serving (half sandwich): 261 calories, 10 g fat, 2 g saturated fat, 7 g protein, 35 g carbs, 3 g fiber, 686 mg sodium

(GF) *Substitute brown rice bread or use brown rice tortillas.*

(V)

Helpful Tip:

To make your own Misto Alla Griglia, slice zucchini and eggplant into ¼-inch-thick pieces, coat with olive oil, and sprinkle with salt and pepper. Grill or pan-sauté until tender.

Chicken in White Wine Sauce

Classic white wine sauce with mushrooms is an intensely flavorful way to serve up chicken. The sauce is made without cream or butter, using broth, garlic, lemon, rosemary, and white wine instead. Crimini mushrooms, which are baby Portobellos, complete the sauce with earthy flavor and meaty texture.

1 lb boneless, skinless chicken breasts or thighs

¼ tsp each salt and black pepper

1 tsp olive oil

1 (8-oz) pkg crimini mushrooms, sliced, or 1 (10-oz) pkg Sliced Crimini Mushrooms

½ cup dry white wine

½ cup chicken broth

2 cloves garlic, crushed, or 2 cubes frozen Crushed Garlic

2-3 sprigs fresh rosemary, plus extra for garnish

4 Tbsp lemon juice, or juice of 1 lemon

1. Sprinkle chicken with salt and pepper. Heat oil in skillet over high heat and brown chicken for 1 minute on each side. Remove chicken breasts and set aside.

2. In the same pan, sauté mushrooms for 2 minutes. Add chicken back to pan. Add wine, broth, garlic, rosemary, and lemon juice. Bring to a boil and allow alcohol to burn off for 2-3 minutes, stirring garlic into sauce. Turn heat to low and cover pan with lid, allowing chicken to simmer for 8 minutes, or until cooked through.

3. Transfer chicken to plates. To thicken sauce, reduce it by simmering with the lid off for a few extra minutes, or stir in 1 Tbsp cornstarch dissolved in 1 Tbsp water. Remove rosemary sprigs and pour sauce over chicken. Garnish with fresh rosemary if desired.

Prep and cooking time: *20-25 minutes*

Serves *4*

NUTRITION SNAPSHOT
Per serving: 184 calories, 6 g fat, 0.5 g saturated fat, 24 g protein, 5 g carbs,
1 g fiber, 318 mg sodium

(GF) ✓

Macadamia-Crusted Mahi Mahi

This classic Hawaiian dish is an island favorite, combining nut-crusted fish with a spicy tropical salsa. Mahi mahi works well here, but you can also use halibut. Serve this dish with Loco for Coconut Rice (page 188) or mashed potatoes.

1 lb mahi mahi, fresh or frozen (thaw if frozen)
Pinch each salt and black pepper
1 Tbsp parsley, chopped finely
1 egg
½ cup macadamia nuts, chopped finely
1 Tbsp oil
1 Tbsp butter
½ cup refrigerated Fire Roasted Papaya and Mango Salsa
Extra parsley for garnish (optional)

1. Pat fish dry using paper towels. Sprinkle salt and pepper on each fillet. If using salted nuts, omit or adjust salt. Rub parsley onto fillets.

2. Beat egg in a small bowl. Place chopped nuts on a plate. Dip each fillet into beaten egg and then press both sides into nuts.

3. Place skillet over high heat and add oil and butter. When hot, add fish and lower heat to medium-high, cooking each fillet for about 2 minutes on each side. If fillets are very thick, preheat oven to 375° F and finish cooking fillets in oven until they are flaky. (If you cook the fish on the stovetop for longer than indicated, the nut coating may burn).

4. Top each fillet with 2 Tbsp salsa and extra parsley.

Prep and cooking time: *15 minutes*

Serves *4*

Variation: *Add ½ cup Panko breadcrumbs to chopped nuts and coat fish with this mixture for a crunchier crust.*

NUTRITION SNAPSHOT
Per serving: 307 calories, 21 g fat, 5 g saturated fat, 24 g protein, 5 g carbs, 1 g fiber, 358 mg sodium

(GF) ✓

Plum Good Stew

Many vegetarian stews are surprisingly rich and hearty. The dried prunes in this stew thicken the sauce and add sweet and sour flavor to the harvest vegetables, accented by the zing of orange and lemon juices. Color and depth come from saffron threads and turmeric. Adding spinach at the end preserves the vibrant green, nicely contrasted against the oranges and yellows. This dish is nice over basmati rice or quinoa and is even better the next day.

2 Tbsp extra virgin olive oil

1 medium onion, chopped, or 1½ cup refrigerated Diced Onions

1 (12- or 16-oz) bag cubed butternut squash (3 cups)

1½ cups orange juice

1½ cups water

8 oz (½ a 16-oz bag) pitted prunes, chopped into quarters

1 (16-oz) bag baby carrots or sliced carrots

1 tsp Spanish Saffron threads (about ½ the jar) or ½ tsp ground saffron

¼ tsp turmeric

½ tsp cinnamon

½ tsp each salt and black pepper

4 Tbsp lemon juice (from 1 large lemon)

1 (6-oz) bag baby spinach

1. Heat oil in a lidded sauté pan and add onion and squash. Cook for 5 minutes, or until onion is soft and squash is slightly browned. Add orange juice, water, prunes, carrots, saffron, turmeric, cinnamon, salt, pepper, and lemon juice.

2. Cover and simmer over low heat for 30-40 minutes, or until stew has thickened. During the last 5 minutes, add spinach and cover. It will seem like a lot of spinach, but it will wilt down quickly.

Prep time: *10 minutes*

Hands-off cooking time: *40 minutes*

Serves 6

NUTRITION SNAPSHOT
Per serving: 194 calories, 5 g fat, 1 g saturated fat, 4 g protein, 45 g carbs, 6 g fiber, 285 mg sodium

(GF) ✓   (V) ✓

Yin Yang Shrimp and Grits

Many shrimp and grits recipes use plenty of cheese and cream, making the dish tasty but quite heavy. This recipe retains all the classic, intense flavors of garlic, wine, and parsley, without the fat. Deana's Southern mother-in-law says that crushed red pepper flakes are a must. Serve the shrimp over polenta, an elegant presentation of traditional grits.

1 lb jumbo uncooked shrimp (peeled, tail on or tail off) thawed if frozen

1½ tsp oil, divided

1 (18-oz) tube pre-cooked Polenta

1 medium onion, diced, or 1½ cups refrigerated Diced Onions

2 cloves garlic, crushed, or 2 cubes frozen Crushed Garlic

½ cup dry white wine

Pinch crushed red pepper flakes (optional)

¼ cup Italian parsley, chopped

Parmesan cheese (optional)

1. Slice polenta into 12 pieces, each ½-inch thick. Heat ½ tsp oil in skillet and pan-fry polenta slices for 3 minutes on each side. Remove polenta and set aside.

2. Add remaining 1 tsp oil to skillet. Add onion and sauté until soft, about 5 minutes.

3. Add shrimp, garlic, wine, and pepper flakes. Cook until shrimp is opaque and firm. Do not overcook shrimp.

4. Remove from heat and stir in parsley. Serve shrimp atop polenta slices, sprinkled with Parmesan.

Prep and cooking time: *20 minutes*

Serves *4 (3 pieces polenta and 6 shrimp per serving)*

NUTRITION SNAPSHOT

Per serving (not including optional garnish): 204 calories, 3 g fat, 0 g saturated fat, 20 g protein, 19 g carbs, 2 g fiber, 504 mg sodium

(GF) ✓

Lime-Marinated Chicken Fajitas

Everyone loves the sizzle of fajitas, the Tex-Mex classic of onions, peppers, and juicy chicken, usually served with warm tortillas and a party of condiments. A lime juice marinade penetrates chicken quickly and adds tangy flavor that brightens the whole dish. Use Trader Joe's ready-made salsas, guacamole, and selection of corn and flour tortillas to make quick work of assembling the spread. Use leftover taco seasoning in our Taco Soup (page 57).

1 lb boneless chicken breasts, sliced thinly (about 2 breasts)

Juice of 1 lime

1 tsp Taco Seasoning

½ tsp salt

1 Tbsp vegetable oil

½ medium onion, sliced thickly

½ each red and yellow bell peppers, sliced, or 1 (8-oz) container pepper strips

1 medium zucchini, cut in half and sliced into ½-inch-thick spears

1. Toss chicken with lime juice, seasoning, and salt, allowing it to marinate while you prepare the vegetables. Marinate chicken for up to 8 hours (refrigerated) for more tender chicken.

2. Heat oil in heavy skillet such as a cast iron pan over highest heat. Add onion and sauté for 2 minutes.

3. Add chicken, allowing it to sear on the pan and cook for 1 minute. Add vegetables and sauté for an additional 3 minutes, or until chicken is cooked through.

Prep and cooking time: *20 minutes*

Serves *4*

NUTRITION SNAPSHOT
Per serving: 185 calories, 8 g fat, 0.5 g saturated fat, 23 g protein, 8 g carbs, 1 g fiber, 456 mg sodium

(GF) ✓

(V) *To make veggie fajitas, omit chicken and increase vegetables. To add protein, substitute sliced seitan or Trader Joe's Chickenless Strips or pair veggie fajitas with brown rice and black beans, a complete protein combination.*

Roasted Red Pepper and Mozzarella Sandwich

You'd expect to see this gourmet sandwich served at a fancy café, but it takes just minutes to make. Roasted peppers taste great right out of the jar and are even better when combined with fresh mozzarella medallions. Serve this sandwich with colorful tomatoes, veggie chips, or fresh fruit for a gourmet lunch in a snap.

1 serving crusty bread, or 1 Organic Miniature Baguette

1-2 pieces Fire Roasted Red or Yellow Bell Peppers

3 pieces Fresh Mozzarella Medallions, or sliced fresh mozzarella cheese

1 tsp balsamic vinegar

4 fresh basil leaves

Salt and black pepper

1. Slice baguette open; toast if desired.

2. Drizzle or brush balsamic vinegar on one side of bread. Layer on roasted red peppers, mozzarella, and basil.

3. Sprinkle with salt and pepper to taste. Close sandwich and serve.

Prep time: *5 minutes*

Serves *1*

NUTRITION SNAPSHOT
Per serving: 248 calories, 9 g fat, 5 g saturated fat, 12 g protein, 29 g carbs, 1 g fiber, 555 mg sodium

(GF) *Use brown rice bread.*

(V) ✓

Spaghetti alla Carbonara

Spaghetti alla Carbonara, a creamy pasta with few ingredients, exemplifies simple Italian cooking. Use pre-cut pancetta mini-cubes or fully cooked bacon as time-saving ingredients in this dish. The creamy sauce is a rich combination of egg yolks and cheese. No cream, butter, or oil is necessary. Serve Carbonara quickly! Connoisseurs serve Carbonara on heated plates to retain the heat and creaminess of the sauce.

1 (16-oz) pkg spaghetti

1 (3.25-oz) pkg Fully Cooked Bacon (10-15 slices), or 1 (4-oz) pkg Cubetti Pancetta (pancetta mini-cubes)

3 egg yolks

⅓ cup grated Parmigiano Reggiano cheese

¼ cup chopped Italian (flat-leaf) parsley

½ tsp black pepper

1. Cook spaghetti according to package instructions.

2. Meanwhile, cut bacon into ½ or 1-inch pieces. Kitchen shears make the job easy. Heat and crisp bacon in pan.

3. Stir together egg yolks and cheese in a large bowl. One Tbsp at a time, stir in 5 Tbsp of boiling pasta water to the mixture to temper eggs and prepare them for the hot pasta. Tempering keeps eggs creamy; shocking them with heat will scramble them.

4. When pasta is done, drain and immediately add to egg mixture and stir vigorously until pasta is coated. Do not rinse pasta before you do this step. Do it quickly so that the intense heat of the pasta cooks the eggs.

5. Stir in bacon, parsley, and pepper. Serve immediately.

Prep and cooking time: *15 minutes*

Serves *8*

Note: *Like other dishes such as Tiramisu and Caesar salad, Carbonara uses raw eggs. The egg yolk heats enough to create a cooked creaminess, but not so much that the egg scrambles.*

NUTRITION SNAPSHOT
Per serving: 313 calories, 6 g fat, 2 g saturated fat, 19 g protein, 52 g carbs, 3 g fiber, 519 mg sodium

(GF) *Substitute brown rice pasta. Brown rice pasta is stickier than regular pasta and may need a little added cream or pasta water to move more freely in the sauce.*

(V) *Substitute vegetarian bacon or sautéed mushrooms for the bacon.*

Baked Gnocchi

Gnocchi are quick-cooking potato dumplings that go well with tomato or cream sauces. We combine the best of both worlds and use Vodka Sauce, a tomato cream sauce. We add peas, basil, and Parmesan and bake the dish to unite the ingredients and crisp the breadcrumb topping.

1 (17.6-oz) bag dry Potato Gnocchi
1 cup Organic Vodka Sauce, or combine ¾ cup marinara with ¼ cup heavy cream
½ cup frozen peas, thawed
2 Tbsp chopped fresh basil
½ cup shredded Parmesan cheese, divided
2 Tbsp bread crumbs

1. Preheat oven to 400° F.
2. Bring salted water to boil and add gnocchi. When gnocchi float to the top, they are done. Drain.
3. In a medium bowl, combine sauce, peas, basil, and ¼ cup Parmesan. Stir in gnocchi.
4. Lightly spray or oil a small casserole dish (8-inch oval). Transfer gnocchi mixture to casserole. Top with remaining cheese and bread crumbs.
5. Bake uncovered for 10 minutes.

Prep time: *10 minutes*

Hands-off cooking time: *10 minutes*

Serves *4*

Variation: *Add cooked pancetta or sausage to casserole before baking.*

NUTRITION SNAPSHOT
Per serving: 285 calories, 13 g fat, 7 g saturated fat, 10 g protein, 33 g carbs, 3 g fiber, 600 mg sodium

Ⓥ ✓

Grilled Lentil Wraps

These wraps are warm and crunchy on the outside, with a moist savory filling on the inside. The crisp outer crust is created by toasting in a cast iron skillet. Dry-toasting (no butter or olive oil necessary) glues the seams together, so grilled wraps don't fall apart like regular wraps do. Serve with your favorite chutney or salsa.

1 small onion, chopped, or 1 cup refrigerated Diced Onions

2 Tbsp olive oil

1 pouch frozen Organic Brown Rice, or 2 cups cooked brown rice

2 cups pre-cooked Steamed Lentils

3 cups frozen spinach (half a 16-oz bag), thawed and excess water squeezed out

¾ cup kefir or plain yogurt

1 cup shredded mozzarella cheese

6 flour tortillas

1. Heat olive oil in a skillet over medium heat. Sauté onion until soft, about 5 minutes. Meanwhile, prepare frozen rice according to package instructions. Add spinach and cook until wilted.

2. Add rice and lentils. Stir until combined and remove from heat.

3. Mix in kefir and cheese.

4. Heat ungreased griddle or skillet over medium heat. Assemble wraps by placing ⅔ cup filling in center of tortilla and folding all sides inward. Place wraps on hot skillet, seam side down. Place a bag of flour or some other heavy object on top to achieve the effect of a panini press. Toast for 3-5 minutes on each side until toasted brown and crispy.

Prep and cooking time: *10 minutes*

Serves *6*

Variations: *Use Swiss chard or any other greens instead of spinach. Substitute other types of cheese such as Havarti, Swiss, or Jack.*

NUTRITION SNAPSHOT
Per serving: 311 calories, 9 g fat, 2 g saturated fat, 13 g protein, 42 g carbs, 6 g fiber, 352 mg sodium

(GF) *Use brown rice tortillas. These are less flexible than regular tortillas, so they need to be heated to soften.*

(V) ✓

Speedy Chicken & Roasted Pepper Quesadillas

Ay caramba! Enjoy flame-grilled flavor in just minutes with these conveniently prepped items begging to go together. Holistic health counselor and regular contributor Marcy Rosenthal saw a version of these flavorful chicken quesadillas demonstrated at her local Trader Joe's. This recipe exemplifies grab-and-go convenience!

1 (12-oz) pkg Grilled Chicken Breast Strips in Chipotle Lime Sauce, or 3 cups cooked chicken

1 (14-oz) bag frozen Fire Roasted Bell Peppers & Onions, thawed

1 (12-oz bag) Fancy Shredded Mexican Blend cheese

8 flour tortillas

Optional dippers and toppings:

Guacamole

Sour cream

Salsa

1. Roughly chop chicken into smaller pieces - thinner filling makes quesadillas bind together better. Mix chicken and roasted peppers in a glass bowl. Microwave for a few minutes to warm chicken mixture. Drain excess liquid.

2. Heat a nonstick/cast iron skillet or griddle over medium heat.

3. Place tortilla in pan and scatter ⅓ cup cheese evenly on entire tortilla. Once cheese begins to melt, place ½ cup chicken mixture on one half and fold tortilla over, pressing to seal. Grill for 1 minute on each side, until quesadillas are lightly browned and crisp on both sides.

4. Cut each quesadilla into 3 wedges and serve with dippers and toppings.

Prep and cooking time: *20 minutes*

Serves *8*

Note: *To bake quesadillas, preheat to 350° F and place assembled quesadillas on a baking sheet. Bake until cheese is melted, about 5-10 minutes.*

NUTRITION SNAPSHOT

Per serving (not including toppings): 355 calories, 15 g fat, 6 g saturated fat, 27 g protein, 31 g carbs, 2 g fiber, 707 mg sodium

(GF) *Use brown rice tortillas.*

(V) *Omit chicken, or substitute Trader Joe's Chickenless Strips.*

Chole and Naan

Komali Nunna, author of _Entertaining from an Ethnic Indian Kitchen,_ shares her quick version of a popular Indian dish, chole. Chole is a simmered combination of garbanzo beans (also called chickpeas) and curry sauce. Using Trader Joe's ready-to-use jarred curry sauce, we capture the taste of long-simmered curry sauce in minutes. Serve chole with Trader Joe's naan, available in multiple flavors in the freezer case or in the bread section.

2 (15.5-oz) cans garbanzo beans, rinsed and drained

1 (15-oz) jar Curry Simmer Sauce or Masala Simmer Sauce

¼ cup chopped red onion

1 tsp – 1 Tbsp finely minced green chiles or jalapeño (optional)

2 Tbsp chopped fresh cilantro

1 Tbsp fresh lime or lemon juice

1. Combine garbanzo beans and curry sauce in a medium saucepan over medium heat. Simmer for 15 minutes. Transfer to a serving dish.

2. Mix onion, chiles, cilantro, and lime. Scatter over garbanzos.

Prep and cooking time: _15 minutes_

Serves _4_

NUTRITION SNAPSHOT
Per serving: 287 calories, 5 g fat, 0 g saturated fat, 14 g protein, 49 g carbs, 14 g fiber, 1041 mg sodium

(GF) _Omit naan serve with rice._

(V) ✓

Ham and Brie Sandwich

Creamy Brie pairs wonderfully with ham and peppery arugula in this sandwich reminiscent of Paris cafés. It's perfect for a gourmet picnic or dinner on your back porch.

1 serving baguette or French bread or 1 Organic Miniature Baguette

1 tsp Aioli Garlic Mustard Sauce

1-2 slices Healthy Ham or your favorite ham

1 oz Brie cheese, sliced

Handful arugula

1. Slice baguette open; toast if desired.

2. Spread mustard on bread. Assemble sandwich with ham, Brie, and arugula.

Prep time: *5 minutes*

Serves *1*

NUTRITION SNAPSHOT
Per sandwich: 270 calories, 10 g fat, 6 g saturated fat, 17 g protein, 27 g carbs, 2 g fiber, 725 mg sodium

(GF) *Use brown rice bread.*

(V) *Substitute roasted red pepper slices for the ham.*

Arugula Pesto Pasta

Pesto, a blend of basil, nuts, Parmesan and olive oil, is a cornerstone of Italian cooking, used generously to add flavor to a wide variety of dishes. We use Trader Joe's ready-made pesto as a dressing in this hearty pasta salad. Chicken sausage and peppery arugula kick up the flavors and textures. Use leftover arugula in our Arugula Salad Pizza (page 177) or Ham and Brie Sandwich (page 144).

12 oz (¾ bag) whole wheat or regular penne pasta

1 (16-oz) pkg Sweet Basil Pesto Chicken Sausage, sliced

1 (8-oz) container refrigerated Genova Pesto, or 1 (8-oz) jar Pesto alla Genovese

3.5 oz (½ pkg) arugula

Shredded or grated Parmesan cheese, for garnish (optional)

1. Boil pasta in salted water, according to package instructions.

2. While pasta is boiling, pan-fry sausage in lightly oiled pan. Although the sausage is fully cooked, pan-frying imparts a nicely browned color.

3. When pasta is cooked, drain. Immediately stir in pesto until noodles are coated.

4. Toss in warm sausage slices and arugula. Heat from the pasta and sausage will slightly wilt arugula.

5. Sprinkle with Parmesan cheese.

Prep and cooking time: *15 minutes*

Serves *6*

NUTRITION SNAPSHOT
Per serving: 409 calories, 24 g fat, 4 g saturated fat, 22 g protein, 26 g carbs, 4 g fiber, 548 mg sodium

(GF) *Substitute brown rice penne.*

(V) *Use vegetarian sausage or omit sausage.*

Easy Chicken Parmigiana

Breaded and fully cooked chicken cutlets take all the prep work out of classic chicken parmigiana. Serve this dish with vegetables or a side of pasta. You can even serve it in a sandwich of panini rolls or pita pockets. This recipe yields plenty for a family, but it's just as easy to make custom portions by heating as many cutlets as desired.

1 (28-oz) bag frozen Breaded Chicken Tenderloin Breasts (~ 12 pieces)
¾ cup no-salt-added Organic Marinara or your favorite pasta sauce
¾ cup shredded mozzarella cheese
¼ cup shredded Parmesan cheese
Fresh basil or parsley

1. Preheat oven to 400° F and bake chicken per package instructions in a 9 x 13-inch baking dish.
2. Meanwhile, heat marinara in a small saucepan.
3. When chicken is done, top each piece with 1 Tbsp marinara, 1 Tbsp mozzarella, and sprinkle of Parmesan. Change oven to broil setting and return chicken until cheese is melted.
4. When serving, garnish with basil.

Prep time: *5 minutes*

Hands-off cooking time: *15 minutes*

Serves *6*

NUTRITION SNAPSHOT
Per serving: 225 calories, 9 g fat, 3 g saturated fat, 20 g protein, 16 g carbs, 1 g fiber, 368 mg sodium

(V) *Substitute frozen Eggplant Cutlets and make eggplant parmigiana.*

Helpful Tip:
Pasta sauce has more complex flavor than plain tomato sauce and is balanced for sweetness and acidity. It's a great all-purpose shortcut in many recipes beyond pasta.

No-Bean Turkey Chili

Not every chili has to feature beans in a headlining role. This satisfying chili gets its heartiness from turkey and vegetables in a smoky and tangy tomato base. Instead of building a sauce from scratch, we use pasta sauce and tweak the flavor profile with cumin and barbecue sauce.

1 (1.4-lb) pkg ground turkey breast or regular ground turkey

1 Tbsp olive oil

1 (14.5-oz) container Mirepoix, or use 1 cup each chopped onions, celery, and carrots

1 (24-oz) jar Rustico Pomodoro Pasta Sauce, or your favorite marinara

1 (14.5-oz) can diced tomatoes with no salt added

¼ cup barbecue sauce

½ tsp cumin

½ cup Fancy Shredded Mexican Blend cheese (optional)

1. Heat oil in sauté pan or pot over medium-high heat. Add mirepoix and sauté 2 minutes. Add turkey, sautéing 4-5 minutes, or until turkey is browned and cooked through, breaking it up as it cooks.

2. Add pasta sauce, tomatoes (including all the juices), barbecue sauce, and cumin.

3. Bring to boil, then lower heat, cover, and simmer for 10-15 minutes, or until carrots are at desired tenderness.

4. Top with a sprinkle of cheese.

Prep time: *10 minutes*

Hands-off cooking time: *15 minutes*

Makes *8 (1-cup) servings*

NUTRITION SNAPSHOT
Per serving: 170 calories, 3 g fat, 0 g saturated fat, 20 g protein, 13 g carbs, 3 g fiber, 551 mg sodium

(GF) ✓

(V) *Substitute 2-3 cups of cooked quinoa or 1 pkg Fully Cooked Wild Rice (reheated according to package instructions) for the cooked ground turkey in step 1.*

Lentil Haystacks

This easy dinner idea comes from Daneen Akers, author of the blog, *Life with Lilybird*. It's based on a taco salad from her childhood called "haystacks." Daneen created a healthy vegetarian version using two of our favorite time-saving products from Trader Joe's – frozen Organic Brown Rice and refrigerated Steamed Lentils, both pre-cooked.

1 (17.6-oz) pkg refrigerated Steamed Lentils

1 Tbsp olive oil

1 medium onion, chopped, or 1½ cups refrigerated Diced Onions

1-2 cloves garlic, crushed, or 1-2 cubes frozen Crushed Garlic

½ cup vegetable or chicken broth

½ cup marinara sauce or tomato sauce

2 pouches frozen Organic Brown Rice, or 4 cups cooked brown rice

Juice of 1 lemon

¼ cup extra virgin olive oil

Your choice of toppings - suggestions include:

Feta cheese	Chopped lettuce
Avocado chunks	Persian cucumbers
Greek olives	Salsa

1. Heat oil in a skillet over medium heat. Sauté onion and garlic until onion is soft, about 5 minutes. Prepare rice while onion is cooking.

2. Add lentils, broth, and marinara to skillet. Cook until lentils are heated through and sauce is combined.

3. Assemble haystacks by putting brown rice in bottom of each bowl. Top with lentils and your choice of toppings.

4. Sprinkle with lemon juice and drizzle with extra virgin olive oil.

Prep time: *15 minutes*

Serves 6

NUTRITION SNAPSHOT

Per serving (not including toppings): 347 calories, 13 g fat, 2 g saturated fat, 10 g protein, 48 g carbs, 8 g fiber, 290 mg sodium

(GF) *Choose gluten-free broth*

(V) ✓

Super-Quick Mushroom Faux-Risotto

Quick risotto? Isn't that an oxymoron? We'll make you a believer with this easy version of risotto, submitted by Susan R. from Los Gatos, CA. Susan writes, "This recipe is super simple, super delicious, and healthy. My 12-year-old daughter loves this and requests it often." The trick is to use Trader Joe's fully cooked frozen brown rice. We playfully named this recipe faux-risotto because the texture isn't as creamy as traditional risotto, but our tasters gave it a thumbs up.

2 pouches frozen Organic Brown Rice, or 4 cups cooked brown rice

1 (10-oz) bag refrigerated Diced Onions, or 1 large onion, chopped

1 (10-oz) pkg Sliced White Mushrooms or Sliced Crimini Mushrooms

2 Tbsp olive oil

2 tsp fresh thyme, or 1 tsp dried thyme

1 cup white wine

⅔ cup shredded Parmesan cheese (preferably Reggiano), plus more for garnish

1. Heat oil in a large skillet. Add onion and sauté until soft, about 5 minutes. Add mushrooms and thyme, and continue cooking until mushrooms are soft, stirring often.

2. While vegetables are cooking, prepare brown rice per package instructions (3 minutes in microwave).

3. Add brown rice to mushroom mixture and stir. Add white wine and cook, stirring frequently, until wine is absorbed. The rice will look like risotto, although the texture will differ. Sprinkle with Parmesan cheese, stir, and cook for a half minute longer, allowing cheese to melt.

4. Sprinkle with additional Parmesan cheese if desired.

Prep and cooking time: *15 minutes*

Serves *4*

NUTRITION SNAPSHOT
Per serving: 213 calories, 6 g fat, 2 g saturated fat, 8 g protein, 32 g carbs, 3 g fiber, 128 mg sodium

GF ✓   V ✓

Eggplant Cutlet Sandwich

Ready-to-use eggplant cutlets take all the work out of preparing eggplant – no salting, breading, or frying. Pair cutlets with fresh mozzarella, basil, and red pepper – all packaged in a crusty panini roll straight out of the oven. We love par-baked breads and rolls at Trader Joe's, but if you prefer, you can use pita to make a pocket sandwich or even lavash bread to make a wrap.

1 Panini Rustic Roll (these are par-baked rolls)

3 frozen Eggplant Cutlets

A few fresh basil leaves

2 slices of fresh mozzarella

1 piece of Fire Roasted Red Pepper (about half a pepper's worth)

1. Place panini in the oven and heat at 400° F until top is golden.

2. Heat eggplant cutlets per package instructions.

3. Slice roll open. Make a sandwich by placing basil leaves on bottom half (this will keep the bread from getting soggy), followed by red pepper, eggplant cutlets, and mozzarella slices.

Prep time: *10 minutes*

Serves *1*

NUTRITION SNAPSHOT
*Per serving: 415 calories, 16 g fat, 5 g saturated fat, 17 g protein,
32 g carbs, 3 g fiber, 651 mg sodium*

Ⓥ ✓

Coq Au Vin

Coq au vin, chicken braised in wine, is a classic French comfort food rich with the flavors and aromas of red wine, mushrooms, and bacon. This traditionally time-consuming dish can be assembled quickly to simmer on the stove, using fully-cooked bacon and pre-sliced mushrooms. Using cooked bacon and skimming excess oil while simmering significantly reduces the fat in this dish while preserving the blast of flavor. Serve over new red potatoes (traditional) or over pasta, quinoa, or rice.

1 (3-lb) pkg bone-in and skin-on chicken pieces (any combination of thighs, breasts, or drumsticks)

½ tsp salt

2 Tbsp olive oil

1 medium onion, sliced, or 1½ cups refrigerated Diced Onions

8 cloves of garlic (available peeled)

3 cups red wine (Burgundy, Pinot Noir, or Zinfandel)

2 cups chicken broth

1 bay leaf

Few sprigs parsley

1 (10-oz) pkg Sliced White Mushrooms

10 slices (⅔ of a 3.25-oz pkg) Fully Cooked Bacon, or cook and drain 10 slices uncooked bacon

1 (1.5-lb) bag new red potatoes or Potato Medley (red, gold, and purple new potatoes)

¼ cup chopped fresh parsley

1. Sprinkle chicken with salt.

2. Heat oil in large pot or deep braising pan. When pot is very hot, add chicken skin side down. Add onion and garlic. Brown chicken for 2-3 minutes on each side. Add wine, broth, herbs, and mushrooms.

3. Cut cooked bacon into ½-inch pieces (kitchen shears work well for cutting bacon quickly) and add to pot. Reduce heat and simmer for 1 hour. Skim surface of any oil.

4. While chicken is simmering, boil potatoes until tender (about 20 minutes).

5. Remove bay leaf. Serve potatoes on the same dish alongside chicken, or roughly mash each potato once with a fork and pour chicken and sauce over potatoes. Top with a sprinkle of parsley.

Prep time: *15-20 minutes*

Hands-off cooking time: *1 hour*

Serves *8*

NUTRITION SNAPSHOT

Per serving: 305 calories, 12 g fat, 3 g saturated fat, 25 g protein, 22 g carbs, 2 g fiber, 716 mg sodium

(GF) *Choose gluten-free chicken broth.*

Salmon Nicoise Salad

Salad Nicoise (knee-SWAZ) from Nice, France is one of the many classic French dishes that Julia Child brought to America. It is traditionally made with canned tuna, but we use salmon for an upscale touch. As a shortcut, use Trader Joe's ready-to-eat hard boiled and peeled eggs, or boil your own (see Helpful Tip on page 47).

1 lb salmon fillets

1 (5-oz) bag salad greens

4 eggs, hard boiled and peeled

1 (8-oz) bag haricots verts (French green beans)

1 lb small potatoes, such as Dutch Gold

2 cups cherry tomatoes or sliced tomatoes

1 cup mixed olives or Kalamata olives

1 (7.4-oz) jar roasted red peppers

1 (12-oz) jar Marinated Artichokes

For Dijon vinaigrette:

2 tsp Aioli Garlic Mustard Sauce, or 1 tsp Dijon mustard + 1 tsp crushed garlic

3 Tbsp white wine vinegar or champagne vinegar

6 Tbsp olive oil

1 tsp salt

1. Preheat oven to broil setting. Lightly spray salmon with oil and sprinkle with salt and pepper.

2. In a large pot with salted water, boil potatoes until fork-tender, about 15 minutes. Broil salmon while potatoes are cooking, about 7 minutes, or until desired doneness. Remove potatoes with a slotted spoon.

3. In the same pot of water, boil haricots verts for 1-2 minutes. Drain and rinse under cold water to stop cooking.

4. Slice eggs in half. Arrange all ingredients on a large platter or assemble individual plates. Drizzle vinaigrette on salad or serve on the side.

Prep and cooking time: *30 minutes*

Serves 8

NUTRITION SNAPSHOT
Per serving: 241 calories, 11 g fat, 2 g saturated fat, 18 g protein, 17 g carbs, 5 g fiber, 474 mg sodium

(GF) ✓

(V) *Use baked tofu instead of salmon. Baked tofu is seasoned and firmer than standard tofu.*

My Big Fat Greek Quiche

This quiche is flavored with the classic elements of a Greek salad – spinach, feta, and tomatoes. Quiche is a versatile around-the-clock meal, appropriate at breakfast, lunch, or dinner. Serve warm or at room temperature, with a simple salad of greens, sliced cucumbers, lemon juice, and olive oil.

1 frozen pie crust, thawed

4 eggs

8 oz (½ bag) frozen chopped spinach, thawed and excess water squeezed out

1 (6-oz) container Crumbled Feta Cheese with Mediterranean Herbs

1 cup chopped tomatoes

1 cup whole milk or half-and-half

¼ tsp black pepper

⅛ tsp ground nutmeg (optional)

1. Preheat oven to 375° F.

2. Place pie crust in a 9-inch pie or quiche pan. Trim and crimp edges. Prick sides and bottom of crust with a fork.

3. Whisk together eggs, milk, pepper, and nutmeg. Add spinach, feta, and tomatoes. Stir gently to combine. Pour egg mixture into crust.

4. Bake for 40 minutes, or until knife inserted in center comes out clean.

Prep time: *10 minutes*

Hands-off cooking time: *40 minutes*

Serves 6

NUTRITION SNAPSHOT
Per serving: 385 calories, 24 g fat, 14 g saturated fat, 15 g protein, 20 g carbs, 2 g fiber, 737 mg sodium

(GF) *Instead of a quiche, make a frittata. Omit the crust, preheat an oven safe skillet in a 350° F oven, and pour the filling in hot skillet. Let frittata continue cooking in oven for 30 minutes or until eggs are set.*

(V) ✓

Spinach & Artichoke Dip Pizza

Warm spinach artichoke dip, a party favorite, is re-purposed in a pizza by using the creamy dip as the sauce. The warm dip goes deliciously with the crisp crust in this creative pizza. Enjoy slices for dinner, or cut the pizza into small bite-size pieces and serve as an easy appetizer.

1 (1-lb) bag refrigerated plain pizza dough

½ container (7 Tbsp) refrigerated Grilled Artichoke & Parmesan Dip

½ (14-oz) can Artichoke Hearts, drained thoroughly and chopped (about ½ cup)

1 cup frozen spinach, thawed

1 cup shredded mozzarella cheese

1. Preheat oven to 500° F or as high as your oven goes.

2. Stretch or roll dough into a 12-inch-diameter circle on a lightly floured surface.

3. Spread artichoke dip on pizza dough. Squeeze water out of thawed spinach. Sprinkle pizza with artichoke hearts, spinach, and cheese.

4. Bake for 8-10 minutes, or until cheese is bubbly.

Prep time: *10 minutes*

Hands-off cooking time: *8-10 minutes*

Serves *4*

NUTRITION SNAPSHOT
Per serving: 384 calories, 12 g fat, 5 g saturated fat, 15 g protein, 51 g carbs, 3 g fiber, 1262 mg sodium

Ⓥ ✓

Summery Shrimp Capellini

Bring the taste of Italy to your dinner table with this simple dish. Cherry tomatoes are pan-roasted to the point of bursting, adding fresh flavor to the shrimp without a lot of sauce. This dish comes together quickly, so have all ingredients at the ready. Mangia!

1 lb uncooked shrimp (peeled, tail on or tail off), thawed if frozen

8 oz (½ pkg) capellini or angel hair pasta

⅓ cup olive oil

4 cloves garlic, crushed, or 4 cubes frozen Crushed Garlic

½ tsp crushed red pepper flakes

1 tsp salt

½ tsp black pepper

1 lb cherry, grape, or sugar plum tomatoes

½ cup chopped fresh basil

½ cup grated Parmesan cheese or Romano/Parmesan blend

1. Cook pasta according to package instructions. Thin pasta cooks quickly, so be vigilant! Drain and place on serving platter. Sprinkle liberally with Parmesan cheese.

2. Heat olive oil in a very large skillet or pan over medium-high heat. Add garlic, red pepper, salt, pepper, shrimp, and tomatoes. Cook for 2-3 minutes until shrimp is opaque and firm. Cook in 2 batches if your pan isn't large enough to accommodate the entire recipe.

3. Add basil to shrimp and toss quickly. Remove from heat and pour over pasta. Serve with additional Parmesan if desired.

Prep and cooking time: *15 minutes*

Serves *4*

NUTRITION SNAPSHOT

Per serving: 466 calories, 23 g fat, 5 g saturated fat, 18 g protein, 49 g carbs, 2 g fiber, 872 mg sodium

(GF) *Substitute brown rice pasta.*

Philly Cheesesteak

This classic sandwich, smothered with onions and peppers, was first invented in Philadelphia as an alternative to hot dogs. Thinly sliced beef is combined with onions and peppers on a fresh roll and topped with melted provolone cheese, considered by many to be the most authentic choice for a cheesesteak. Serve with our Garlic Baked Sweet Potato Fries (page 215).

1 (1-lb) pkg Flat Iron Beef Chuck Steak
2 Tbsp olive oil
1 large onion, thinly sliced
1 large green bell pepper, thinly sliced
1 baguette loaf, cut into 6 pieces, or 6 hoagie rolls
6 slices provolone cheese

1. Preheat broiler.
2. Heat olive oil in large skillet over medium-high heat. Add onion and green pepper and sauté until soft. Remove from heat and set aside.
3. Cook beef in same pan to desired doneness. Allow beef to rest for 10 minutes, and then slice thinly on a diagonal against the grain.
4. Divide onion and pepper mixture among rolls. Divide beef among rolls. Halve provolone slices and place on top of assembled sandwiches.
5. Place under broiler for 5 minutes to melt cheese and warm sandwiches.

Prep and cooking time: *20 minutes*

Serves *6*

NUTRITION SNAPSHOT
Per serving: 380 calories, 21 g fat, 8 g saturated fat, 25 g protein, 24 g carbs, 2 g fiber, 493 mg sodium

(GF) *Substitute brown rice bread or a brown rice tortilla.*

(V) *Substitute 4 Portobello mushrooms for the steak. Slice mushrooms and sauté with peppers and onions.*

Sloppy Joe's

A Sloppy Joe recipe seems only appropriate in a cookbook about our favorite Joe. This all-American kid-friendly classic consists of a saucy ground meat filling, rich with tangy barbecue flavors, served on a hamburger bun. It's meant to be messy, but if you're nervous about picking it up, it's ok to use a fork. Serve with Creamed Spinach (page 216) for a gourmet cafeteria-style blowout.

1 lb 93% lean ground beef or turkey

1 Tbsp olive oil

1 small onion, chopped, or 1 cup refrigerated Diced Onions

1 small green or red bell pepper, chopped (about 1 cup)

2 cloves garlic, crushed, or 2 cubes frozen Crushed Garlic

2 cups no-salt-added marinara or 1 (18-oz) bottle Traditional Marinera (convenient size but higher sodium content)

¼ cup ketchup

3 Tbsp barbecue sauce

2 Tbsp chopped parsley

4 hamburger buns, Honey Whole Wheat Hamburger Buns (toast if desired)

1. Heat olive oil in a pan over medium-high heat. Add onion, pepper, and garlic. Cook for 5 minutes.

2. Add beef, breaking it up as it cooks, and cook until no red pieces are visible. Drain or scoop off excess fat.

3. Add marinara, ketchup, and barbecue sauce. Stir to mix and continue cooking until sauce is incorporated and thickened, about 2 minutes longer.

4. Remove from heat and sprinkle on parsley. Serve between hamburger buns.

Prep and cooking time: *15 minutes*

Serves *4*

NUTRITION SNAPSHOT
Per serving: 547 calories, 18 g fat, 1 g saturated fat, 40 g protein, 54 g carbs, 7 g fiber, 670 mg sodium

(GF) *Substitute brown rice bread or a brown rice tortilla, or serve nacho-style over corn tortilla chips.*

(V) *Substitute an equivalent amount of crumbled tempeh or firm tofu for the beef. To give tofu a meatier texture that crumbles easily, freeze and thaw tofu before cooking.*

Tamale Bake

Inspired by tamales, this quick and easy casserole features polenta, the Italian version of Southern grits. Polenta is firm and crumbly when cold, but is transformed into soft layers of chewy goodness when heated. Using pre-cooked polenta sold in formed tubes makes this delicious casserole a snap. Experiment with other vegetables such as butternut squash, bell peppers, or eggplant, and other cheeses such as goat cheese, to create a myriad of tasty variations.

2 (18-oz) tubes pre-cooked polenta, each tube sliced into 9 rounds

2 Tbsp olive oil

1 large onion, chopped, or 2 cups refrigerated Diced Onions

3 zucchini squash, sliced

1 (12-oz) pkg Soy Chorizo, removed from casing, or substitute 1 lb ground meat cooked in 1 tsp Taco Seasoning or ⅓ cup Enchilada Sauce

2 (15-oz) cans black beans, drained

½ cup Enchilada Sauce

1 cup Fancy Shredded Mexican Blend cheese

¼ cup fresh cilantro, chopped

Sour cream as garnish (optional)

1. Preheat oven to 350° F.

2. Heat olive oil in a skillet. Sauté onion and zucchini until soft, about 5 minutes. Add chorizo and stir. Remove from heat.

3. Lightly oil a 9 x13-inch baking pan (or use an 8 x 8-inch pan if making half a batch). Place half the polenta on the bottom, overlapping as necessary. Sprinkle on half each of the chorizo mixture, black beans, enchilada sauce, and shredded cheese. Repeat with the 2nd layer.

4. Cover and bake for 30 minutes until cheese is melted and casserole is piping hot. Sprinkle cilantro evenly on top. Serve with sour cream.

Prep time: *20 minutes*

Hands-off cooking time: *30 minutes*

Serves *10*

NUTRITION SNAPSHOT
Per serving (not including garnish): 294 calories, 12 g fat, 4 g saturated fat, 15 g protein, 35 g carbs, 10 g fiber, 1084 mg sodium

(GF) ✓ (V) ✓

Mediterranean Baked Fish

Classic Mediterranean flavors and colors add boldness to mild white fish in this easy entrée. We use readily available tilapia, but any white fish such as cod or sole works well. White wine keeps the fish from drying out and makes a delicious sauce for dipping bread or pouring over rice.

1 lb tilapia, thawed if frozen (4 fillets)

1 cup cherry tomatoes, halved, or chopped Roma tomatoes

¼ cup chopped Kalamata olives

½ small onion, chopped, or ½ cup refrigerated Diced Onions

2 cloves garlic, crushed, or 2 cubes frozen Crushed Garlic

2 Tbsp chopped parsley

2 Tbsp olive oil

¼ cup white wine

½ tsp salt

1. Preheat oven to 375° F.

2. Place fish in a single layer in an 8 x10-inch baking dish.

3. In a bowl, mix tomatoes, olives, onion, garlic, and parsley. Spoon mixture evenly over fish.

4. Whisk oil, wine, and salt. Pour evenly over entire dish. It won't seem like enough liquid, but more juices will be released during cooking.

5. Bake uncovered for 25 minutes, or until fish flakes easily.

Prep time: *10 minutes*

Hands-off cooking time: *25 minutes*

Serves *4*

NUTRITION SNAPSHOT

Per serving: 211 calories, 11 g fat, 2 g saturated fat, 24 g protein, 4 g carbs, 1 g fiber, 419 mg sodium

(GF) ✔

Arugula Salad Pizza

Pizzas in Italy are nothing like the pizzas here, as we have learned from our Italian friends who introduced us to salad-topped pizza. A simple cheese pizza makes the base for a lemony and peppery arugula salad in our version. A Caesar or Greek salad also goes well on top of a warm pizza. For the best crust using a pizza stone, see our Helpful Tip on page 165.

1 (1-lb) bag refrigerated pizza dough, whole wheat or plain

2 tsp olive oil

1½ cups Quattro Formaggio shredded cheese

Salad topping:

3.5 oz (half bag) arugula salad leaves

1 Tbsp lemon

2 Tbsp olive oil

2 Tbsp pine nuts (optional)

1. Preheat oven to 500° F or as high as your oven goes.

2. Stretch or roll pizza dough to a 12-14 inch-diameter circle on a lightly floured surface.

3. Brush top with olive oil and sprinkle cheese on top.

4. Bake for 8-10 minutes, or until cheese is bubbly.

5. Whisk lemon juice, and olive oil in a mixing bowl. When pizza is done, toss arugula with dressing. Scatter arugula salad on top of pizza. Top with pine nuts.

Prep time: *10 minutes*

Hands-off cooking time: *8-10 minutes*

Serves *4*

Note: *If you like garlic, mix 1 clove crushed garlic with olive oil in step 3, and then brush pizza dough with this mixture.*

NUTRITION SNAPSHOT
Per serving: 477 calories, 27 g fat, 9 g saturated fat, 21 g protein, 51 g carbs, 2 g fiber, 410 mg sodium   Ⓥ ✔

Herbed Citrus Shrimp with Quinoa and Goat Cheese

Citrus zest, fresh herbs, and tangy goat cheese are a lively combination in this shrimp and quinoa dish brought to us by Tracy Holleran, owner and instructor of The Secret Ingredient cooking school. For citrus zest, make sure to buy fragrant fruits (best in winter when citrus is in season); aim for organically-grown fruit since you will be eating the peel.

1 lemon

1 orange

1 lime

2 Tbsp olive oil, divided

¼ tsp salt

2 Tbsp each chopped fresh mint and parsley, divided

1 lb large uncooked shrimp (peeled and tail off), thawed if frozen

1 cup quinoa

2 oz goat cheese, broken into small chunks, or Crumbled Goat Cheese

2 Tbsp fresh basil, cut into thin ribbons

1. Zest orange, lemon, and lime, and then juice each. In a large bowl, whisk together citrus juices, 1 Tbsp olive oil, salt, and 1 Tbsp each parsley and mint. Reserve 2 Tbsp of this marinade for adding to the finished dish. Add shrimp to juice mixture and allow to marinate for 15 minutes.

2. Meanwhile, rinse quinoa and cook according to package instructions.

3. In a skillet over high heat, add 1 Tbsp olive oil. Using a slotted spoon, remove shrimp from marinade and place in pan. Discard used marinade. Cook 1 minute per side, until shrimp is opaque and firm. Do not overcook shrimp.

4. Toss shrimp with cooked quinoa, and add remaining fresh mint and parsley. Drizzle with reserved marinade, add goat cheese, and toss to combine. Garnish with basil ribbons and sprinkle with citrus zest mixture.

Prep and cooking time: *25 minutes*

Serves *4*

NUTRITION SNAPSHOT
Per serving: 336 calories, 12 g fat, 3 g saturated fat, 27 g protein, 32 g carbs, 3 g fiber, 400 mg sodium

(GF) ✔

(V) *Omit shrimp and substitute cubed firm tofu. It's a great idea to marinate tofu in a flavorful marinade such as the one here since tofu has little flavor on its own*

Helpful Tip:
If the thought of crunching into an occasional undercooked onion makes you shudder, sauté onions first before adding to meatloaf mixture.

Mom's Meatloaf

Right up there with mac-and-cheese, this is one of America's best-loved comfort foods. Equally good hot out of the oven or cold in a sandwich, this classic is a cinch to prep. Don't skip the brown sugar and ketchup glaze – it makes the meatloaf!

1 (1-lb) pkg 93% lean ground beef or turkey

1 egg, lightly beaten

½ cup oats or breadcrumbs

1 small onion, finely chopped, or 1 cup refrigerated Diced Onions

⅓ cup beef broth, chicken broth, or milk

¼ cup chopped parsley

1 tsp salt

⅓ cup ketchup

3 Tbsp brown sugar

2 tsp Dijon or yellow mustard

1. Preheat oven to 350° F.
2. In a bowl, mix beef, egg, oats, onion, broth, parsley, and salt until well combined. Use your hands and mix gently because aggressive mixing can make the meat tough.
3. Shape mixture into a mound on a lightly oiled cookie sheet, or place into a lightly oiled 5 x 9-inch loaf pan. Mix ketchup, brown sugar, and mustard. Spread this glaze evenly over top of meatloaf.
4. Bake for 45 minutes, or until juices run clear.

Prep time: *10 minutes*

Hands-off cooking time: *45 minutes*

Serves *6*

NUTRITION SNAPSHOT
Per serving: 214 calories, 9 g fat, 3 g saturated fat, 18 g protein, 16 g carbs, 2 g fiber, 407 mg sodium

(GF) *Use oats tested for gluten content. Choose gluten-free broth.*

Did you know? *Experts say the best way to bake meatloaf is on a cookie sheet, allowing meat to bake instead of steam. We think the biggest advantage of baking on a cookie sheet is covering more of the meatloaf's surface with glaze, everyone's favorite part of the dish.*

Simple Sides

Give Peas a Chance

Poor green peas, always relegated to boring cafeteria fare and never invited to the fancy dinners. This recipe brings an upscale flair to English peas, combining them with crisp, flavorful pancetta and sautéed onions. Pancetta is an Italian cured meat, similar to bacon but without the smokiness. Trader Joe's sells it conveniently cubed and ready to use.

1 (1-lb) bag frozen peas, thawed
1 (4-oz) pkg Cubetti Pancetta (pancetta mini-cubes)
½ medium onion, sliced thinly
¼ tsp black pepper (optional)
Shredded Parmesan cheese for garnish (optional)

1. Heat a skillet over high heat. No oil is necessary. Sauté pancetta for 3 or 4 minutes until crisp. Transfer pancetta to a plate, leaving rendered fat in the pan.

2. In the same pan, sauté onion until soft, about 5 minutes.

3. Add peas to pan and cook only until heated through (1-2 minutes). Add pancetta back into pan, sprinkle with pepper, and toss. Transfer contents to serving bowl, and top with a sprinkle of Parmesan.

Prep and cooking time: *15 minutes*
Serves *6*

Variation: *Use crumbled bacon in place of pancetta.*

NUTRITION SNAPSHOT
Per serving (not including garnish): 147 calories, 9 g fat, 3 g saturated fat, 6 g protein, 11 g carbs, 4 g fiber, 236 mg sodium

(GF) ✔

(V) *Omit pancetta and instead sprinkle with Crumbled Feta, vegetarian bacon, or Parmesan to add saltiness and texture.*

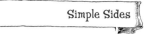

Roasted Cauliflower with Olives

It was common decades ago to boil the life out of cauliflower, leaving it mushy and tasteless. Enter the new age of roasted cauliflower – a simple and incredibly delicious dish that will forever change the way you think about this vegetable. Roasting at high heat brings out cauliflower's natural sweetness, balanced here by salty Kalamata olives. If you skip the olives, sprinkle lightly with salt, or add grated Parmesan cheese after roasting. This is a rustic dish that's equally good as an appetizer or side.

1 (12-oz) pkg Cauliflower Florets, or 4 cups cauliflower cut into florets
4 tsp olive oil
½ tsp 21 Seasoning Salute, or your favorite seasoning
½ cup Kalamata olives, about a dozen

1. Preheat oven to 400° F.

2. Toss cauliflower with olive oil. Sprinkle with seasoning and stir to coat. Mix in olives.

3. Place cauliflower mixture on baking sheet, spreading in a single layer. Roast for 20 minutes, flipping halfway through baking time to roast evenly. Cauliflower will be crisp-tender. For softer cauliflower, continue roasting for an additional 10 minutes.

Prep time: *5 minutes*

Hands-off cooking time: *20 minutes*

Serves 6

NUTRITION SNAPSHOT
Per serving: 58 calories, 4 g fat, 1 g saturated fat, 2 g protein, 5 g carbs, 2 g fiber, 381 mg sodium

(GF) ✓   (V) ✓

Loco for Coconut Rice

Enjoy this delicate coconut rice with fish, Thai dishes, or Indian curries. Coconut milk gives ordinary rice a hint of exotic flavor and a creamy and silky texture without a lot of added fat and calories. Add extra coconut milk near the end of cooking time to achieve a creamy risotto-like texture.

1 cup jasmine rice
1 cup water
1 cup light coconut milk
¼ tsp salt

1. In a medium saucepan, combine rice, water, coconut milk, and salt.

2. Bring mixture to a boil. Reduce heat and cover, simmering 15 minutes, or until all water is absorbed. Remove from heat and allow to rest for 5 minutes, then fluff with fork.

Prep time: *2 minutes*

Hands-off cooking time: *20 minutes*

Serves *4*

NUTRITION SNAPSHOT
*Per serving: 210 calories, 3 g fat, 2 g saturated fat, 3 g protein, 41 g carbs,
0 g fiber, 163 mg sodium*

(GF) ✓   (V) ✓

99 LBS. NET WEIGHT
WHOLE BEAN
UNCOATED
TABLE RICE

Irish Soda Bread

Soda bread is a staple in Irish cuisine, served at breakfast, lunch, and dinner. This version with raisins is mildly sweet and perfect for breakfast or afternoon tea. Quick breads are easy to make because you simply mix and bake; no kneading or rising is required. Sour cream and eggs make this bread more moist than traditional soda bread, a quality that may offend die-hards. This recipe makes one large loaf. Alternatively, split the dough in two and make an extra loaf to share with a friend or neighbor.

3½ cups flour
¼ cup sugar
1 tsp baking soda
1 tsp salt
1 cup raisins
2 eggs
1 (16-oz) container light or regular sour cream (2 cups)

1. Preheat oven to 375° F.
2. Mix flour, sugar, baking soda, and salt in a large bowl. Add raisins and mix them in with your fingers, making sure raisins separate and are coated with flour. This prevents raisins from clumping in the dough.
3. In a separate bowl, whisk eggs, then add sour cream and combine. Add wet mixture to flour mixture and stir with a wooden spoon until just combined. Dough will be sticky, like biscuit dough. Do not overmix, as this will result in tough bread.
4. Dust your hands with flour and lightly shape dough into a circular mound, approximately 8 inches wide. Use a gentle touch; do not knead or handle dough too much. Transfer to a lightly oiled or lined baking sheet (Silpat baking mats work well), and cut a big X on top. The X allows heat to penetrate bread and cook more evenly; it also gives homemade bread a professional look.
5. Bake for 45 minutes, or until lightly browned and toothpick inserted in center comes out clean. If splitting dough into 2 loaves, check for doneness at 35 minutes.

Prep time: *15 minutes*

Hands-off cooking time: *45 minutes*

Serves *16*

Sweet variations: *Substitute cranberries, currants, or dried blueberries for the raisins.*

Savory variations: *Reduce sugar to 2 Tbsp, omit raisins, and instead use 1 Tbsp caraway seeds or 1 cup sunflower seeds.*

NUTRITION SNAPSHOT
Per serving: 202 calories, 4 g fat, 2 g saturated fat, 5 g protein, 37 g carbs, 1 g fiber, 253 mg sodium

Ⓥ ✓

Almond Bread

Almond meal is a slightly more coarse version of almond flour, made of ground almonds with the skin left on. We use it to make delicious and healthy almond bread that is low carb, high protein, and gluten-free. This bread was inspired by a recipe from Elana Amsterdam at the *Elana's Pantry blog*. We love the nutty taste and moist, hearty texture. Enjoy plain or topped with cream cheese and honey.

1 (16-oz) bag Just Almond Meal (about 4½ cups)

1 tsp salt

1 tsp baking soda

1 Tbsp baking powder

5 large eggs

2 Tbsp agave nectar

½ cup plain yogurt such as Plain Cream Line Yogurt

1 tsp sesame seeds (optional)

1. Preheat oven to 325˚ F.
2. In a large bowl, combine almond meal, salt, baking soda, and baking powder.
3. In a medium bowl, whisk together eggs, agave nectar, and yogurt.
4. Add wet mixture to dry mixture and mix thoroughly.
5. Pour mixture into a 5 x 9-inch oiled loaf pan and sprinkle with sesame seeds.
6. Immediately place in oven on center rack and bake for 55 minutes, or until a toothpick inserted in center comes out clean. If top begins to brown too much, drape with foil. When cool, run a sharp knife along edge of pan to loosen bread and remove to slice.

Prep time: *10 minutes*

Hands-off cooking time: *55 minutes*

Serves *12*

NUTRITION SNAPSHOT
Per serving: 317 calories, 25 g fat, 2 g saturated fat, 13 g protein, 11 g carbs, 5 g fiber, 450 mg sodium

GF ✓   V ✓

Sweet Potatoes with Balsamic Maple Glaze

The natural sweetness of sweet potatoes is set off by the flavorful tang of a balsamic maple glaze. Sweet potatoes are tasty and easy to cook; we haven't met anyone yet, kids included, who does not love them. This delicious root vegetable also packs a nutritious punch. Sweet potatoes are full of dietary fiber, natural sugars, vitamin C, beta carotene, and Vitamin A.

1 (16-oz) bag Cut Sweet Potatoes (or peel and cut your own ¾-inch cubes, about 3 cups worth)

3 Tbsp vegetable oil, divided

3 Tbsp maple syrup, divided

5 Tbsp peeled and minced shallots (~3 shallots)

2 Tbsp balsamic vinegar

¼ tsp each salt and pepper

1. Preheat oven to 400° F.

2. In a medium bowl, toss sweet potatoes with 2 Tbsp oil and 2 Tbsp maple syrup until coated. Transfer sweet potatoes onto a lightly oiled baking sheet. Spread them out so that they roast evenly.

3. Roast sweet potatoes in oven for 20-25 minutes, or until fork-tender, tossing halfway through.

4. While sweet potatoes are roasting, sauté shallots in a small saucepan with 1 Tbsp oil until shallots are soft. Add balsamic vinegar and remaining 1 Tbsp maple syrup. Simmer over low heat for about 5 minutes until sauce is slightly reduced and thickened. Remove from heat.

5. Remove sweet potatoes from oven and transfer to medium serving bowl. Drizzle with sauce and toss to coat.

Prep time: *10 minutes*

Hands-off cooking time: *25 minutes*

Serves *4*

NUTRITION SNAPSHOT
Per serving: 206 calories, 11 g fat, 1 g saturated fat, 1 g protein, 27 g carbs, 2 g fiber, 187 mg sodium

(GF) ✓ (V) ✓

Easy Spanish Rice

This Spanish rice recipe is so easy that you may never buy a boxed mix again. Use your favorite salsa to flavor rice with a natural combination of tomato, pepper, onion, herbs, and spices. Serve as a savory side to Mexican dishes or use as a base for paella.

1 cup rice
1 Tbsp oil
½ cup Chunky Salsa, or your favorite salsa
1 cup chicken or vegetable broth
1 cup water

1. In a medium saucepan over medium-high heat, combine rice and oil, stirring until rice is coated and hot. Add remaining ingredients and stir to combine.

2. Bring to boil, cover, and reduce heat. Simmer for 20 minutes, or until all water is absorbed. Fluff with fork.

Prep time: *5 minutes*

Hands-off cooking time: *20 minutes*

Serves *4*

NUTRITION SNAPSHOT
Per serving: 218 calories, 4 g fat, 0 g saturated fat, 5 g protein, 40 g carbs, 2 g fiber, 214 mg sodium

(GF) *Choose gluten-free broth.*

(V) *Use vegetable broth.*

Harvest Glazed Carrots

The natural sweetness of carrots is enhanced when they are cooked, making them a colorful side dish with lots of family appeal. Here, we add some instant autumn flair using pumpkin butter as an easy stir-in glaze for the carrots. With the added crunch of pecans and the sweetness of plump raisins, these glazed carrots are a no-fuss, easy addition to any meal.

3 cups sliced carrots, or 1 (16-oz) bag baby carrots

2 Tbsp Pumpkin Butter, available seasonally

¼ cup raisins

¼ cup chopped pecans

1. Boil or steam carrots until crisp-tender.

2. Drain carrots and place into a serving bowl. Stir in pumpkin butter, raisins and pecans.

Prep and cooking time: *10-15 minutes*

Serves *4*

NUTRITION SNAPSHOT
Per serving: 130 calories, 5 g fat, 0 g saturated fat, 2 g protein, 23 g carbs, 4 g fiber, 67 mg sodium

(GF) ✓   (V) ✓

Cranberry Pomegranate Fresca

This raw cranberry relish is fantastic spooned onto pork or grilled chicken breast. Pomegranate arils are the perfect sweet "crunch" in every bite of this fresh-tasting and tangy relish. It's also a tasty alternative to traditional cooked cranberry sauce.

1 (12-oz) pkg whole cranberries
3 Tbsp Lemon Curd, or ⅓ cup sugar + 1 Tbsp lemon juice
½ cup fresh pomegranate arils ("seeds" from half a pomegranate)

1. Chop cranberries in a food processor or a blender. Be careful to pulse, and only chop roughly.
2. Transfer to bowl and add lemon curd, stirring to distribute evenly.
3. Stir in pomegranate seeds.
4. If using sugar and lemon, let relish sit for an hour before serving. If you like it sweeter, sprinkle on a little extra sugar. Don't add more lemon curd or it will get too gooey.

Prep time: *10 minutes*
Makes *12 (¼-cup) servings*

NUTRITION SNAPSHOT
Per serving: 41 calories, 0 g fat, 0 g saturated fat, 0 g protein, 11 g carbs, 2 g fiber, 1 mg sodium

(GF) ✓   (V) ✓

Couscous with Sun Dried Tomatoes

The flavors of Tuscany come alive with this easy dish of whole wheat couscous. Couscous is a terrific side because it takes only minutes to prepare and goes well in place of rice or pasta. Marinated artichokes and sun dried tomatoes add sweet and savory flavor and are easy pantry items to keep on hand. Add any combination of fresh herbs or even goat cheese or feta. To make this dish an entrée, add bite-size pieces of Just Chicken (pre-cooked charbroiled chicken).

1½ cups dry Whole Wheat Couscous
1 (12-oz) jar Marinated Artichokes; do not drain
½ (8.5-oz) jar Julienne Sliced Sun Dried Tomatoes, drained completely
1 cup water
¼ cup chopped fresh basil

1. Pour liquid from jar of artichokes into a medium saucepan. Roughly chop artichokes.

2. To the saucepan, add chopped artichokes, tomatoes, and water. Bring to a boil.

3. Stir in couscous, remove pan from heat, and cover for 5 minutes until water is absorbed. Fluff, stir in basil, and serve.

Prep and cooking time: *10 minutes*

Serves *6*

NUTRITION SNAPSHOT
Per serving: 282 calories, 10 g fat, 1 g saturated fat, 8 g protein, 41 g carbs, 5 g fiber, 381 mg sodium

(GF) *Omit couscous. Substitute cooked quinoa.*

(V) ✓

Butternut Squash Quinoa

One of our readers, Debbie F., sent us this recipe using one of our favorite ingredients, quinoa. Quinoa is packed with more protein than any other grain, is a vegetarian source of the complete set of essential amino acids, and is a great alternative to rice. Garlicky butternut squash complements the nutty taste of quinoa. Debbie says that her cousins ask for this recipe at all their gatherings. This dish can be served warm or cold.

1 (12-oz) pkg Cut Peeled Butternut Squash, diced into smaller pieces (about 3 cups)

2 Tbsp olive oil

½ tsp salt

¼ tsp black pepper

1 tsp garlic powder

½ cup chopped onion or refrigerated Diced Onions

1 cup quinoa, rinsed

2 cups vegetable or chicken broth

2 Tbsp butter

⅛ cup dried cranberries (optional)

⅛ cup dried apricots, chopped (optional)

1. Preheat oven to 350° F.

2. Place butternut squash on a baking sheet. Pour olive oil over squash and toss to coat. Sprinkle with salt, pepper and garlic powder, and toss again. Spread seasoned squash in a single layer and bake for 15 minutes.

3. Add onion and bake for another 10 minutes.

4. Transfer cooked vegetable mixture to a medium pot and add quinoa, broth, and butter. Bring mixture to a boil. Cover, reduce heat, and simmer for 15 minutes, or until water is absorbed.

5. Stir in dried cranberries and dried apricots.

Prep time: *5 minutes*

Hands-off cooking time: *40 minutes*

Serves *4*

NUTRITION SNAPSHOT
Per serving: 306 calories, 15 g fat, 3 g saturated fat, 7 g protein, 37 g carbs, 4 g fiber, 573 mg sodium

(GF) *Choose gluten-free broth.*

(V) ✓

Roasted Asparagus with Tomatoes and Feta

Dress up asparagus with ripe tomatoes and savory feta cheese. Roasting preserves the fresh green color and crisp texture of asparagus, unlike steaming, which can yield a stringy washed-out vegetable. This colorful dish is an elegant accompaniment to any meal, especially one with an Italian, Mediterranean, or Greek theme.

1 (12-oz) pkg fresh asparagus spears
2 tsp olive oil
⅛ tsp salt
1 tomato, sliced
1 Tbsp Crumbled Feta
⅛ tsp black pepper

1. Preheat oven to 400° F.

2. On baking sheet, toss asparagus with oil until well coated. Line up asparagus in a single layer, sides touching. Sprinkle lightly with salt.

3. Place sliced tomatoes in a row along the center. Sprinkle feta cheese and pepper evenly on top.

4. Bake for 10 minutes until asparagus is crisp-tender. For softer asparagus, cook 5-10 minutes longer.

Prep time: *10 minutes*

Hands-off cooking time: *15 minutes*

Serves 6 *(about 3 spears per person)*

NUTRITION SNAPSHOT
Per serving: 42 calories, 3 g fat, 1 g saturated fat, 2 g protein, 4 g carbs, 2 g fiber, 71 mg sodium

(GF) ✓   (V) ✓

French Dressed Green Beans

Baby French green beans, known as haricots verts, are prized for their delicate texture and velvety skin. The traditional French way to serve haricots verts is lightly dressed with a mustard-flavored sauce. Trader Joe's garlic aioli mustard makes it a breeze to summon this classic French flavor out of a bottle.

1 (8-oz) bag haricots verts, or 2 cups frozen haricots verts

2 tsp Garlic Aioli Mustard Sauce

2 tsp olive oil

1. Bring a pot of salted water to a boil and add green beans. After water returns to a boil, cook for 3 minutes. Remove green beans and plunge into a large bowl filled with ice water to stop the cooking. Drain completely.

2. Whisk mustard sauce and oil in a large bowl. Add green beans and toss to coat.

Prep and cooking time: *10 minutes*

Serves *4*

NUTRITION SNAPSHOT
Per serving: 42 calories, 3 g fat, 0 g saturated fat, 1 g protein, 2 g carbs, 2 g fiber, 31 mg sodium

(GF) ✓   (V) ✓

Artichoke-Stuffed Portobellos

Portobello mushrooms have a meaty texture and earthy flavor that is a nice backdrop to a flavorful filling made of artichoke hearts and bruschetta sauce. Fresh Bruschetta Sauce, a fresh-tasting blend of tomatoes, basil, and garlic, is one of our favorite Trader Joe's products. This dish takes just moments to put together, cooks quickly in the oven, and is a versatile side. It can shine as an entrée if paired with a salad or simple pasta.

4 portobello mushroom caps, stems removed

1 (14-oz) can artichoke hearts

1 cup refrigerated Fresh Bruschetta Sauce

½ cup bread crumbs

½ cup shredded Parmesan cheese

Basil, cut into ribbons (optional)

1. Preheat oven to 400° F.

2. Drain artichoke hearts. Roughly chop artichoke hearts and drain again, pressing lightly to remove more water. Combine artichoke hearts with bruschetta sauce, bread crumbs, and Parmesan.

3. Divide mixture between portobello caps and press lightly to compact filling.

4. Place portobellos on oiled baking sheet face up and cook for 12-14 minutes. As soon as you see water being released, remove from oven and serve immediately. Garnish with basil.

Prep time: *5 minutes*

Hands-off cooking time: *12-14 minutes*

Serves *4*

Variation: *Make risotto-stuffed portobellos. Prepare Trader Joe's frozen risotto according to package instructions, stir in pine nuts or chopped walnuts for texture, and use as stuffing mixture. Bake as before.*

NUTRITION SNAPSHOT

Per serving: 169 calories, 4 g fat, 2 g saturated fat, 9 g protein, 21 g carbs, 5 g fiber, 399 mg sodium

(GF) *Substitute almond meal or cooked rice for bread crumbs.*

(V) ✓

Black Bean and Mango Salad

Eating legumes is easy when they are presented attractively. Papaya and mango salsa brings a vibrant touch to an otherwise colorless dish and adds a fruity kick. This particular salsa is spicy – be forewarned! Substitute a milder salsa for less heat. This flavorful salad goes well with chicken or pork and has plenty of fiber from both black beans and wild rice.

2 (15-oz) cans black beans, rinsed and drained
1 (15-oz) container refrigerated Fire Roasted Papaya Mango Salsa
1 (16-oz) bag fully cooked Wild Rice, or 3 cups cooked wild rice

1. Prepare wild rice according to package instructions. Place rice in a mixing bowl and fluff with a fork.
2. Add salsa and black beans. Toss well and serve.

Prep time: *5 minutes*

Serves *8*

NUTRITION SNAPSHOT
Per serving: 186 calories, 1 g fat, 0 g saturated fat, 9 g protein, 36 g carbs, 8 g fiber, 780 mg sodium

(GF) ✓   (V) ✓

Baked Garlic Sweet Potato Fries

Fries that are both flavorful and healthy? Yes, it's not an oxymoron when you use sweet potato spears baked with garlic and seasonings. Substitute these tasty and nutritionally superior fries for traditional French fries and watch them disappear.

1 (12-oz) bag Sweet Potato Spears
2 Tbsp olive oil
2 cloves garlic, crushed, or 2 cubes frozen Crushed Garlic, thawed
¼ tsp salt
⅛ tsp black pepper

1. Preheat oven to 400° F.
2. Place olive oil, garlic, salt, and pepper in a mixing bowl. Whisk until combined.
3. Add sweet potatoes and mix until spears are evenly coated.
4. Place potatoes in a single layer on a baking sheet. Bake for 20-25 minutes, flipping halfway for even browning.

Prep time: *5 minutes*

Hands-off cooking time: *20-25 minutes*

Serves *4*

NUTRITION SNAPSHOT
Per serving: 134 calories, 7 g fat, 1 g saturated fat, 1 g protein, 17 g carbs, 3 g fiber, 192 mg sodium

(GF) ✓ (V) ✓

Dreamy Creamed Spinach

There's good reason mom always said to eat your spinach – it's full of calcium to strengthen bones; vitamins, fiber, and folic acid to fight cancer; folate to prevent heart disease; flavonoids to protect against memory loss. It's hard to believe that something so good for you can taste so good too. This nutritious superhero basking in a luscious creamy sauce is bound to become a family favorite side, perfectly paired with roast chicken, juicy steak, or even macaroni-and-cheese. This side will do double duty for everyday meals as well as holiday feasts.

1 (16-oz) pkg frozen spinach, thawed and excess water squeezed out

1 Tbsp olive oil

1 Tbsp butter

½ cup finely chopped onion

2 cloves garlic, crushed, or 2 cubes frozen Crushed Garlic

2 Tbsp flour

1½ cups milk

1½ cups chicken or vegetable broth

⅛ tsp nutmeg (optional)

½ cup grated Parmesan cheese

1. Heat olive oil and butter in a sauté pan over medium heat.

2. Add onion and sauté until soft, about 5 minutes. Add garlic and cook 1 minute longer.

3. Add flour and stir, cooking for 1 minute.

4. Add milk, broth, nutmeg, and spinach. Stir to combine. When mixture comes to a boil, reduce heat, cover, and simmer for 10 minutes.

5. Stir in Parmesan and remove from heat.

Prep and cooking time: *20 minutes*

Serves *6*

NUTRITION SNAPSHOT
Per serving: 144 calories, 8 g fat, 3 g saturated fat, 10 g protein, 11 g carbs, 2 g fiber, 358 mg sodium

(GF) *Substitute 1 Tbsp cornstarch for the flour. Choose gluten-free broth.*

(V) *Use vegetable broth.*

Sesame Toasted Sugar Snap Peas

Sugar snap peas are delicious on their own and can be eaten raw. The less you do to them, the better, to let their crunchy sweet taste shine. Here we make the peas glisten with just a smidge of nutty sesame oil. A quick burst of heat enhances their naturally sweet flavor and vibrant color. Do not overcook.

1 (12-oz) bag Sugar Snap Peas or snow peas
1 tsp toasted sesame oil
Pinch salt
2 Tbsp water
1 tsp sesame seeds

1. Heat skillet or wok over medium-high heat.

2. Mix peas, sesame oil, and salt in a mixing bowl until evenly coated.

3. Toss peas into skillet. Add water and quickly stir-fry for 2-3 minutes until water evaporates and peas are bright green and still crisp.

4. Remove from heat and sprinkle with sesame seeds.

Prep and cooking time: *5 minutes*

Serves *4*

NUTRITION SNAPSHOT
Per serving: 49 calories, 2 g fat, 0 g saturated fat, 2 g protein, 6 g carbs, 2 g fiber, 39 mg sodium

(GF) ✓ (V) ✓

Delicious Desserts & Daring Drinks

Sunflower Butter Cookies

These easy sunflower butter cookies are a tasty variation on traditional peanut butter cookies. They're sweet, dense, nutty, and slightly chewy, just the way these cookies should be. Sunflower butter is an alternative for people who are allergic to peanut butter or simply prefer its taste. If you want to stick with tradition, peanut butter will work just as well.

1 (16-oz) jar Sunflower Butter (about 1¾ cups) at room temperature
1 cup sugar
2 eggs
1 tsp vanilla
1 pinch salt

1. In a medium bowl, mix together sunflower butter, sugar, eggs, vanilla, and salt until smooth. Dough will slightly thicken after being mixed together.

2. Refrigerate for about 1 hour.

3. Preheat oven to 350° F.

4. Scoop walnut-size portions of dough, lightly roll in hands, and place on a lightly oiled or lined baking sheet (Silpat baking mats work well). Dough will be soft but holds together without being sticky. Place cookies about 1-2 inches apart, as they will not spread much.

5. Make imprints on top of cookies with a fork. If the fork sticks, dip fork in sugar or sprinkle a tiny bit of sugar on each cookie before pressing fork into it.

6. Bake for 12 minutes. Don't overbake these cookies! Allow cookies to cool before removing from baking sheet.

Prep time: *10 minutes*

Hands-off cooking time: *12 minutes*

Makes *30 cookies*

Note: *Sunflower butter turns dark green when the naturally occurring chlorogenic acid (a desirable antioxidant) in sunflower seeds meets baking soda. These cookies don't contain baking soda, so they won't turn green, but you will notice the effect in recipes that do, a great coincidence when baking for holidays like St. Patrick's.*

NUTRITION SNAPSHOT
Per cookie: 116 calories, 8 g fat, 1 g saturated fat, 4 g protein, 10 g carbs, 2 g fiber, 65 mg sodium

(GF) ✓ (V) ✓

"A Hint of Coffee" Brownies with Café Latte Glaze

Adding a touch of coffee to chocolate desserts intensifies the chocolate flavor and takes it to a new level. We adapted our recipe from an espresso brownie recipe by Giada De Laurentiis. We use Trader Joe's rich brownie mix, adding a touch of coffee flavor using instant coffee and drizzles of a café latte glaze.

1 (16-oz) pkg Brownie Truffle Baking Mix (plus 2 eggs and 1 stick butter to prepare mix)
2 Tbsp instant coffee

Café Latte Glaze:

1 Tbsp instant coffee
1 Tbsp water
½ tsp vanilla
1 Tbsp butter at room temperature
⅔ cup powdered sugar

1. Prepare brownies according to instructions, but when mixing together butter and eggs, whisk in instant coffee. Bake and cool completely.

2. To prepare glaze, combine coffee, water, vanilla, and butter, whisking to combine. Slowly whisk in powdered sugar, little by little, until glaze is thick but still pourable. Drizzle over entire pan of brownies, or cut brownies into pieces and drizzle over each piece. Place in fridge until glaze sets.

Prep time: *15 minutes*

Hands-off cooking time: *25-30 minutes*

Serves *16*

Variation: *Use Trader Joe's Mini Milk Chocolate Peanut Butter Cups to create a gooey chocolate-peanut-butter version. After preparing the Brownie Truffle Baking Mix, stir in 1 cup peanut butter cups into the batter and bake as directed.*

NUTRITION SNAPSHOT
Per serving: 222 calories, 9 g fat, 5 g saturated fat, 2 g protein, 22 g carbs, 1 g fiber, 59 mg sodium

(GF) *Substitute Trader Joe's Gluten-Free Brownie Mix.*

(V)

Snappy Rice (&) Pudding

We like making our own rice pudding because we can customize it with our own spices and flavorings. However, we don't particularly care for the hour of cooking time or the mess when the rice pudding invariably boils over onto the stovetop. To make an instant "homemade" warm rice pudding, we combine frozen rice and instant pudding. The rice is slightly chewier than conventional rice pudding but our kids prefer it.

1 pouch frozen Organic Jasmine Rice, or 2 cups cooked rice

1 (4-oz) pkg Vanilla Instant Pudding (plus 2 cups cold milk)

½ tsp cinnamon

Optional toppings or add-ins: citrus zest, candied ginger, chopped dates, dried berries, nuts

1. Heat rice according to package instructions (3 minutes in microwave). Open bag slightly, add ¼ cup water to rice and microwave for additional 30 seconds.

2. In a large bowl, add milk and pudding mix, stirring until smooth. Add rice and stir to combine. Transfer to individual bowls or into a large serving bowl.

Prep time: *5 minutes*

Serves *6*

Variation: *Use chocolate pudding mix.*

NUTRITION SNAPSHOT
Per serving: 167 calories, 2 g fat, 1 g saturated fat, 4 g protein, 35 g carbs, 0 g fiber, 304 mg sodium

(GF) ✓   (V) ✓

Orange Creamsicle Smoothie

Remember those yummy orange Creamsicles we all loved as kids? This creamy smoothie captures the creamy orange and vanilla essence of those beloved popsicles in a healthy morning smoothie. If you don't like using ice in smoothies, or if your blender can't blend ice, simply substitute a second cup of mango for the cup of ice.

1 cup Vanilla Nonfat Yogurt
1 cup orange juice
1 cup frozen Mango Chunks
1 cup crushed ice
1 tsp vanilla

1. Add all ingredients to blender and blend until smooth.
2. Pour into glasses and garnish with an orange slice.

Prep time: *5 minutes*
Makes *2 (1½-cup) servings*

Note: *Vanilla Nonfat Yogurt is a sweetened yogurt. If you prefer to use plain yogurt, add agave nectar or sugar for a sweeter taste.*

NUTRITION SNAPSHOT
Per serving: 172 calories, 0 g fat, 0 g saturated fat, 6 g protein, 36 g carbs, 2 g fiber, 52 mg sodium

(GF) ✓ (V) ✓

Monkey Bread

Yes, it's so 1960's, but it's so darn good. Monkey bread is a lazy version of cinnamon rolls or sticky buns, often served for brunch but decadent enough to qualify as dessert. Usually made with bread dough that needs to rise before baking, our version uses buttermilk biscuits, which can be baked right away. Monkey bread is a yummy gooey pastry that doesn't make any pretense about being a diet food. It is infinitely better when enjoyed warm, straight out of the oven.

2 (16-oz) cans refrigerated Buttermilk Biscuits

½ cup sugar

2 tsp cinnamon

6 Tbsp butter

½ cup brown sugar

2 Tbsp maple syrup

⅓ cup chopped nuts (optional)

¼ cup raisins (optional)

1. Preheat oven to 350˚ F.

2. Mix sugar and cinnamon in a large bowl. Cut biscuits into fourths and toss biscuit pieces in cinnamon sugar until each piece is coated.

3. If using nuts and raisins, sprinkle several spoonfuls into the bottom of a Bundt pan. Arrange biscuit pieces in pan, sprinkling remaining nuts and raisins as you go along. Pour any remaining cinnamon sugar into pan.

4. Melt butter and brown sugar in a small saucepan, stirring until dissolved. Remove from heat and stir in maple syrup. Pour this mixture evenly over biscuits.

5. Bake for 35-40 minutes, or until browned. Invert immediately onto a serving plate, letting the sticky syrup pour out (otherwise syrup will harden on bottom of pan). Serve immediately.

Prep time: *15 minutes*

Hands-off cooking time: *35-40 minutes*

Serves *12*

Note: *If you don't have a Bundt pan, use a 9 x13-inch pan, or halve the recipe and bake in an 8- or 9-inch round pan, reducing cooking time to ~25 minutes.*

NUTRITION SNAPSHOT
Per serving (not including nuts or raisins): 302 calories, 8 g fat, 4 g saturated fat, 5 g protein, 54 g carbs, 1 g fiber, 669 mg sodium   (V) ✔

Bellini

The Bellini is one of Italy's most popular cocktails, originating in Venice. Traditionally made with Prosecco sparkling wine and white peach purée, it's a refreshing, fruity, and light drink perfect for summer days and celebrations. We use peach juice, conveniently adding summer sweetness.

⅔ cup Prosecco, chilled
⅓ cup Dixie Peach juice or other peach nectar, chilled

1. Add peach juice to highball glasses or champagne flutes.
2. Add Prosecco and serve immediately. Do not stir or the drink will fall flat.

Prep time: *2 minutes*
Serves *1*

Note: *1 bottle of Prosecco serves 4*

NUTRITION SNAPSHOT
Per serving: 85 calories, 0 g fat, 0 g saturated fat, 0 g protein, 11 g carbs, 0 g fiber, 9 mg sodium

(GF) ✓ (V) ✓

Lemon Ricotta Almond Cake

This twist on cheesecake is made with almond meal, capturing the essence of classic Italian desserts. It combines the richness of almonds, the sweetness of ricotta, and the zing of lemon. No other flour is used, making it healthy and gluten-free. Serve with a small dollop of whipped cream or top with extra lemon zest.

2 cups Just Almond Meal
1 tsp baking powder
¼ tsp salt
3 large eggs
1 cup sugar
1 tsp vanilla
1 (15-oz) container ricotta cheese (2 cups)
Zest of 1 lemon
Juice of 1 lemon (about 3 Tbsp)

1. Preheat oven to 350° F.
2. In a large bowl, combine almond meal, baking powder, and salt.
3. In a medium bowl, combine remaining ingredients and mix well.
4. Add wet ingredients to dry ingredients and stir well until smooth.
5. Pour mixture into oiled 9-inch pan, deep pie dish, or springform pan. Bake 55-60 minutes until cake is completely puffed up, no longer "jiggly" in the center, and very golden on the edges.
6. Cool cake completely (it will deflate) and thoroughly chill in fridge for at least 4 hours before serving. Cake remains moist and is better the next day. Serve with whipped cream or garnish with lemon zest.

Prep time: *10 minutes*

Hands-off cooking time: *55-60 minutes*

Serves *12*

NUTRITION SNAPSHOT
Per serving: 261 calories, 14 g fat, 4 g saturated fat, 10 g protein, 23 g carbs, 2 g fiber, 156 mg sodium

(GF) ✓   (V) ✓

Did you know? *Almonds are a great source of protein, vitamin E, monounsaturated (good) fats, magnesium, phosphorus, zinc, calcium, folic acid and fiber.*

Helpful Tip:
The lemon zest adds so much to this
cake – choose a fresh, fragrant lemon
and make sure you use only the outer
peel, avoiding the bitter white pith.
Use a microplane grater for tiny flecks
of zest, or a citrus zester if you want
larger strips of lemon as a garnish
(shown in photo). Both tools are
inexpensive and good additions to
your kitchen drawer.

Chocolate Truffle Pie with Joe-Joe's Crust

The votes are in. Deana's two young kids announced, "Mom, this is the best dessert you've ever made." The chocolate filling is firm and silky, and uses only two ingredients. The chocolate crust is easy and made with crushed Trader Joe's Joe-Joe's cookies.

Crust:

28 Joe-Joe's Cookies with Vanilla Bean filling (2 rows out of the package)

¼ cup melted unsalted butter

Filling:

1 (12-oz) bag semi-sweet chocolate chips

1 (14-oz) can light coconut milk

1. Preheat oven to 350° F.

2. Crush cookies in a food processor. Pulse until cookies are fine crumbs. Pour in melted butter and pulse until combined. Press crumbs firmly into an oven-safe pie dish and up the sides, using the bottom of a glass or a measuring cup to apply pressure and form crust.

3. Bake crust for 5 minutes. Remove from oven and cool completely.

4. Melt chocolate, either on stovetop or in microwave. (Microwave method: Place chips in a small glass bowl and microwave for 1 minute and then in 30 second increments, stirring well in between until completely smooth and melted. Do not scorch.)

5. Pour coconut milk into a blender and add melted chocolate. Blend immediately, until mixture is completely smooth, about 20-30 seconds.

6. Pour filling into crust and chill for 4 hours or overnight in fridge.

Prep and cooking time: *15-20 minutes, not including cooling/chilling time*

Serves *12*

Variation: *Use Trader Joe's "Instant Chocolate Pudding" mix to fill the pie. The texture and taste is that of eating a thick classic chocolate pudding rather than a silky chocolate truffle. If you make a pudding filling, use two boxes pudding mix and 3 cups cold whole milk.*

NUTRITION SNAPSHOT

Per serving: 341 calories, 21 g fat, 10 g saturated fat, 2 g protein,
43 g carbs, 2 g fiber, 155 mg sodium

Ⓥ ✓

Lemon Drop Martini

The Lemon Drop became popular in 1970's California and has since earned a spot as a classic favorite drink, combining lemony flavors with the kick of vodka. Both Simple Syrup and agave nectar dissolve easily in cold liquids, making this an easy drink to mix. If using sugar instead, use a shaker to dissolve.

2 oz vodka (4 Tbsp)

½ oz triple sec or limoncello (1 Tbsp)

1 oz fresh lemon juice (2 Tbsp), saving a wedge or the peel for garnish

2 tsp Simple Syrup or 1 tsp agave nectar

1-2 Tbsp sugar (optional, for the rim)

1. Place sugar in a shallow dish. Rub rim of a martini glass or short tumbler with lemon and dip into sugar.

2. Fill glass with ice cubes and add vodka, triple sec, lemon juice, and simple syrup, stirring gently to combine.

Prep time: *5 minutes*

Serves *1*

NUTRITION SNAPSHOT
Per serving: 211 calories, 0 g fat, 0 g saturated fat, 0 g protein, 14 g carbs, 0 g fiber, 0 mg sodium

(GF) ✓   (V) ✓

Very Cherry Crumble

Jarred sweet tart and pitted cherries combine with pecan-studded and maple-sweetened granola for a simple but rich dessert. Serve warm, casually spooned into bowls, and top with ice cream, whipped cream, or Greek yogurt.

1 (24.7-oz) jar Dark Morello Cherries
2 cups Pecan Praline Granola
1 Tbsp flour

1. Preheat oven to 375° F.

2. Drain and reserve cherry juice from jar of cherries.

3. In an 8 x 8-inch buttered or oiled baking dish, add cherries (drained) and sprinkle with 1 Tbsp flour, stirring to coat. Stir in 1 cup reserved cherry juice and spread cherries evenly in dish.

4. Spread granola over cherries.

5. Bake uncovered for 10-15 minutes.

Prep time: *10 minutes*

Hands-off cooking time: *10-15 minutes*

Serves *8*

NUTRITION SNAPSHOT
Per serving: 183 calories, 4 g fat, 0 g saturated fat, 3 g protein, 34 g carbs, 2 g fiber, 30 mg sodium

(GF) *Substitute corn starch for flour. Substitute oats or gluten-free granola for regular granola. Gluten-free granola tends to get soggy more quickly so serve dessert immediately after baking.*

(V) ✓

Cinnamon Bread Pudding

Trader Joe's Cinnamon Swirl Bread is so good that it rarely lasts long enough to make this warm, comforting dessert. We cube this wonderful bread and add a touch of honey and cream to make bread pudding. To keep the texture soft and delicate, use a water bath in the oven (see explanation below). Enjoy bread pudding warm and optionally top with ice cream, a drizzle of heavy cream, or a little mascarpone cheese mixed with sugar and cinnamon.

5 slices Cinnamon Swirl Bread, cubed (about 6 cups worth)

3 eggs

1 cup half-and-half

¼ cup honey

½ tsp cinnamon

1 tsp sugar

Six 6-oz ramekins (these are the smaller 3.5-inch ones)

1. Preheat oven to 350° F.

2. In a medium bowl, whisk together eggs, half-and-half, and honey.

3. Add bread cubes and let them soak for 10 minutes. Do not stir since that will create a mush. Once or twice, using a large spoon or spatula, gently flip bread cubes over so that the mixture soaks in evenly.

4. Divide mixture among 6 well-buttered or oiled ramekins. Press gently to compact slightly. Combine cinnamon and sugar and sprinkle on top.

5. Place ramekins in a baking dish and fill outer baking dish with hot water until water is halfway up the sides of ramekins.

6. Place in oven (carefully!), drape with foil, and bake for about 30 minutes until bread pudding is firm in the center.

Prep time: *15 minutes*

Hands-off cooking time: *30 minutes*

Serves 6

NUTRITION SNAPSHOT
Per serving: 293 calories, 10 g fat, 4 g saturated fat, 8 g protein, 44 g carbs, 0 g fiber, 144 mg sodium

Ⓥ ✓

Did you know? *Egg-based dishes such as custards and bread puddings need to be cooked gently since the proteins can bind and get tough if cooked with high, direct heat. The hot water bath (also called a bain-marie) keeps the heat a bit more mild and moist than the direct heat of being placed on an oven rack.*

Helpful Tip:
When measuring honey, first spray measuring cup or spoon with a little cooking oil. Honey will slide right off.

Maple Whipped Cream

When you're looking for a luscious, lightly sweetened topping that isn't overloaded with sugar, try whipped cream. Maple syrup adds a hint of distinctive flavor to whipped cream without overpowering it. Use real maple syrup for best flavor; imitation pancake syrups with high fructose corn syrup won't taste the same. This topping is terrific on pancakes or waffles, on pumpkin pie, or as an alternative to frosting on carrot cake.

1 cup heavy cream
¼ cup maple syrup

1. Pour cream and maple syrup into a mixing bowl. Beat with a mixer on high speed until stiff peaks form. Do not overmix, or cream will turn into butter.

2. Use as you would whipped cream or light frosting. Store in fridge until ready to serve.

Prep time: *5 minutes*

Makes *2 cups whipped cream*

NUTRITION SNAPSHOT
*Per tablespoon: 42 calories, 4 g fat, 2 g saturated fat, 0 g protein,
2 g carbs, 0 g fiber, 4 mg sodium*

(GF) ✓   (V) ✓

Helpful Tip:
If using as frosting, be sure to completely cool the baked item before frosting. Heat will make whipped cream melt.

Creamy Chai

One of our readers describes chai with milk as "a warm hug," and we agree. Trader Joe's Ruby Red Chai is an aromatic blend of tea and spices, made even better with honey and almond milk. Smooth and sweet, perfect for morning or evening.

1 teabag Ruby Red Chai
1 tsp honey
1 Tbsp Unsweetened Vanilla Almond Milk

1. Prepare tea with 1 cup boiling water.
2. Sweeten with honey (if desired, add more to taste).
3. Add almond milk as you would add milk to coffee.

Prep time: *5 minutes*

Serves *1*

NUTRITION SNAPSHOT

Per serving: 29 calories, 0 g fat, 0 g saturated fat, 0 g protein, 7 g carbs, 0 g fiber, 10 mg sodium

(GF) ✓   (V) ✓

Baked Pearfection

Baked pears are an elegant dessert, rich with aromas of vanilla, honey, and spice. It's traditional to bake pears in Brandy, but here we use Drambuie, a scotch whisky liqueur from the Isle of Skye. Drambuie is sweet, infused with spices and herbs, and adds depth of flavor to the pears and sauce. If you don't have Drambuie, substitute brandy for the classic version of this dessert.

2 pears (Bosc are best for baking, but most pears in season will work)
1 Tbsp butter
2 Tbsp honey
1 tsp vanilla
2 Tbsp Drambuie
¼ cup Candied Pecans or Candied Walnuts (optional)

1. Preheat oven to 375° F.

2. Peel and halve pears. Use a spoon to remove cores. Arrange pear halves, cut side up, on an oven safe dish.

3. In a small saucepan over medium heat, combine butter, honey, vanilla, and Drambuie. When mixture is warm and butter has melted, remove from heat. Brush mixture onto all sides of each pear half, and then pour mixture onto pears, letting excess liquid run off sides into baking dish. Set saucepan aside for further use. Drape baking dish with foil and bake pears for 20 minutes.

4. Plate pears, leaving any liquid in baking dish. Pour liquid into the same saucepan and reduce over medium-low heat for 5 minutes until liquid is syrupy.

5. When serving, sprinkle with a few pecans and spoon syrup over each pear.

Prep time: *10 minutes*

Hands-off cooking time: *20 minutes*

Serves *4*

NUTRITION SNAPSHOT
Per serving (not including nuts): 129 calories, 3 g fat, 2 g saturated fat, 0 g protein, 23 g carbs, 3 g fiber, 2 mg sodium

(GF) ✓   (V) ✓

Good-for-you Strawberries and Cream

Silky and rich, Greek yogurt fills in for whipped cream in this variation of classic strawberries and cream. Adding just a bit of sugar to strawberries causes juices to release, creating a sweet, syrupy concoction in just minutes. The longer you leave the strawberries, the juicier they will become.

1 cup strawberries, diced or sliced
1 tsp brown sugar
½ cup plain Greek yogurt
1 tsp honey
1 tsp lemon juice

1. Toss together strawberries and sugar. Set aside for 10 minutes.
2. Combine yogurt, honey, and lemon juice. Pour over strawberries. Drizzle extra honey if desired.

Prep time: *10 minutes*

Serves *1*

NUTRITION SNAPSHOT
*Per serving: 217 calories, 10 g fat, 6 g saturated fat, 6 g protein,
29 g carbs, 3 g fiber, 58 mg sodium*

Low-Fat Wide Awake Coffee Shake

Love coffee? This low-fat version of a thick coffee shake uses nonfat plain frozen yogurt, deliciously tangy and not too sweet. Chocolate covered espresso beans add sweet crunch and an intense burst of coffee and chocolate flavor. Similar shakes typically use vanilla or coffee ice cream, which has a whopping 600+ calories per 1-cup serving, and half of those are fat calories. The nonfat frozen yogurt used in this recipe has ⅓ the calories and zero fat, making this a guiltless treat.

2 cups Nonfat Plain Frozen Yogurt
⅓ cup water with 1 Tbsp instant coffee dissolved in it, or ⅓ cup cold strong coffee
12 Dark Chocolate Covered Espresso Beans (about ¼ cup)

1. Combine all ingredients in a blender and blend until smooth. Adjust the amount of liquid to get the consistency you like.

2. Pour into tall glasses and serve immediately.

Prep time: *5 minutes*

Serves *2*

NUTRITION SNAPSHOT
Per serving: 265 calories, 2 g fat,
1 g saturated fat, 9 g protein, 52 g carbs,
0 g fiber, 121 mg sodium

(GF) ✓ (V) ✓

Chocolate Lava Cake

Chocolate Lava Cake is a brownie-like cake with a warm pudding center that oozes out when cut. For chocolate lovers, this is heaven on a plate. It's been said this cake was invented by mistake, when a baker forgot to put flour in the cake batter. We think it's one of the best mistakes in baking history. Although Trader Joe's sells ready-made frozen chocolate lava cake, this homemade version adapted from Jean-George Vongerichten's classic is superior, and it really doesn't take much effort. Serve with fresh fruit or vanilla ice cream.

½ cup (1 stick) butter, plus extra for buttering the molds

4 oz dark/bittersweet chocolate, preferably Valrhona**

2 eggs

2 egg yolks

¼ cup sugar

1 tsp instant coffee, dissolved in ½ tsp hot water (optional)

2 Tbsp flour, plus a little more for dusting the molds

Powdered sugar for garnish (optional)

Four (4-oz) ramekins or molds

1. Preheat oven to 450° F.
2. Break up chocolate into pieces in a glass mixing bowl. Cut up butter into chunks and add to chocolate. Melt chocolate and butter over a double-boiler or in the microwave (use 30-second intervals, stirring in between) until chocolate is melted. Whisk to combine.
3. Whisk eggs, egg yolks, sugar, and coffee in a small bowl. Pour egg mixture into melted chocolate and stir well. Add flour and stir just until combined. Do not overmix.
4. Butter ramekins and dust with flour, shaking out excess. Divide batter evenly among molds.
5. Place ramekins on a baking tray and bake for 6-7 minutes, or until sides are set. The center will be soft and look undercooked (see photo on next page).
6. Wait for 10 seconds before inverting molds onto serving dishes. After inverting, sprinkle lightly with powdered sugar. Serve immediately.

Prep and cooking time: *15-20 minutes*

Serves *4*

**Valrhona is widely acknowledged as the premium chocolate bar for bakers. If you're making this dessert for a large crowd, Trader Joe's Pound Plus dark chocolate is an acceptable substitute and offers a great value.

NUTRITION SNAPSHOT
Per serving (not including garnish): 508 calories, 40 g fat, 23 g saturated fat, 8 g protein, 8 g carbs, 10 g fiber, 48 mg sodium

(V) ✓

Cake is done when sides are set and center is still soft

Helpful Tip:

To invert molds, run a knife along sides to loosen cake. Place serving plate over mold. Using oven mitts, hold plate firmly against mold and quickly invert. Lightly tap mold until cake releases. Remove mold and serve.

Mighty Mojito

The mojito is a classic Cuban drink that balances strong rum with sweetness, fresh lime juice, and cool mint leaves. This refreshing drink is served over crushed ice and typically enjoyed as a popular warm-weather drink. Don't chop the mint leaves or they will muddy the drink with mint specks. Instead, bruise mint leaves to release the intoxicating aroma and oils.

8-10 mint leaves

2 Tbsp fresh lime juice

2 oz rum (¼ cup)

1 tsp honey or agave nectar

⅔ cup French Market Limeade or other lime soda

1 cup crushed ice

1. Place mint leaves in a glass, tearing large leaves in two. Add lime juice. Use a muddler or wooden spoon to crush mint leaves against glass and release juices.

2. Add rum and honey. Stir well.

3. Add lime soda and crushed ice. Stir again and garnish with additional mint leaves and lime slices if desired.

Prep time: *5 minutes*

Serves *1*

NUTRITION SNAPSHOT
Per serving: 228 calories, 0 g fat, 0 g saturated fat, 1 g protein, 26 g carbs, 1 g fiber, 26 mg sodium

(GF) ✓   (V) ✓

Nearly Instant Homemade Mango Ice Cream

Yes, it's possible to make ice cream at home without an ice cream maker and in just minutes! The trick is to combine frozen fruit and half-and-half (or heavy cream) in a food processor. The result is a soft ice cream, made with any fruit flavor you like. Although the texture is not identical to commercial ice cream, the flavor is outstanding, and it just can't get simpler to make ice cream.

12 oz (about half the bag) Frozen Mango Chunks
⅔ cup half-and-half
¼ cup sugar

1. Combine half-and-half and sugar and stir for 30 seconds until sugar starts to dissolve.

2. Do not thaw mango; for this recipe it should be frozen hard. Add frozen mango to a food processor, and process just to chop it up roughly. Add half-and-half and process until mixture is smooth (1-2 minutes).

3. Serve right away. Or, for a hard-frozen ice cream, pour into a freezer-safe container and place in freezer for about 2 hours. Stir it every 30 minutes until it freezes, helping to break up ice crystals that may form.

Prep time: *5 minutes*

Makes *4 (½-cup) servings*

Variation: *Use frozen strawberries or any other frozen fruit instead of mango. Experiment with unusual fruits and combinations for unique ice creams all your own! For a richer ice cream, substitute heavy cream.*

NUTRITION SNAPSHOT
Per serving: 157 calories, 5 g fat, 3 g saturated fat, 2 g protein, 27 g carbs, 1 g fiber, 17 mg sodium

(GF) ✓   (V) ✓

Helpful Tip:
Cleaning up caramel is easier than you think. Just soak in water, and the hardened caramel will dissolve for easy cleanup.

You Can Flan!

Flan is a creamy custard baked with a layer of caramel. Wona grew up eating flan in Venezuela and loves all types – coconut, coffee, pumpkin, and even lavender. The caramel topping is the perfect accompaniment to the lusciously creamy custard. The caramel used for flan is very basic - just burnt sugar. Some caramel-type desserts feature caramel that is overly sweet. Not so with flan. The caramel is light and runny. Traditionally, flan is made with heavy cream, but we found that whole milk works just as well. For a more luxurious flan, use 2 cups half-and-half.

¾ cup sugar

5 eggs

1 (14-oz) can sweetened condensed milk, available seasonally

2 cups whole milk

2 tsp vanilla

Pinch salt

1. Preheat to 350° F with rack in middle of oven. Place 8-inch or 9-inch round pan in oven to warm; a warm pan will prevent caramel from hardening too quickly.

2. In a heavy saucepan, melt sugar over medium-low heat, stirring occasionally. When sauce is deep amber, like the color of maple syrup, remove from heat. Pour into warmed pan, tilting quickly to coat pan. Be nimble, because the caramel hardens quickly. Don't worry if caramel layer isn't perfectly smooth — it will melt as flan cooks.

3. Whisk together eggs and condensed milk until well blended. A blender works well, in batches. Add milk, vanilla, and salt. Blend until combined. Pour this mixture on top of hardened caramel.

4. Create a water bath by placing flan into a larger baking dish. Pour boiling water into outer dish until water level reaches halfway up sides of flan. Bake for 1 hour, or until knife inserted in center comes out clean. Don't worry if flan doesn't look completely set; as long as it passes the knife test, it's done.

5. Remove flan from heat, cool, and chill in fridge for 8 hours or overnight. When ready to serve, slide a knife around edges of pan to release flan. Place serving plate on top of pan, and invert flan quickly while holding plate firmly against pan. Remove pan, let caramel pour out, and serve.

Prep and cooking time: *15 minutes*

Additional hands-off cooking time: *1 hour*

Serves *12*

NUTRITION SNAPSHOT
Per serving: 247 calories, 7 g fat, 4 g saturated fat, 7 g protein, 39 g carbs, 0 g fiber, 126 mg sodium

(GF) ✓   (V) ✓

Index

No-Gluten Recipe Index

Recipes that are No-Gluten or can easily be made No-Gluten (*) using simple substitutions

Appealing Appetizers

Soups & Salads

Main Meals

Vegetarian Recipes Index

Recipes that are Vegetarian or can be made Vegetarian (*) using simple substitutions

Trader Joe's Store Locations

ARIZONA

Ahwatukee # 177
4025 E. Chandler Blvd., Ste. 38
Ahwatukee, AZ 85048
Phone: 480-759-2295

Glendale # 085
7720 West Bell Road
Glendale, AZ 85308
Phone: 623-776-7414

Mesa # 089
2050 East Baseline Rd.
Mesa, AZ 85204
Phone: 480-632-0951

Paradise Valley # 282
4726 E. Shea Blvd.
Phoenix, AZ 85028
Phone: 602-485-7788

Phoenix (Town & Country) # 090
4821 N. 20th Street
Phoenix, AZ 85016
Phone: 602-912-9022

Scottsdale (North) # 087
7555 E. Frank Lloyd Wright
N. Scottsdale, AZ 85260
Phone: 480-367-8920

Scottsdale # 094
6202 N. Scottsdale Road
Scottsdale, AZ 85253
Phone: 480-948-9886

Surprise # 092
14095 West Grand Ave.
Surprise, AZ 85374
Phone: 623-546-1640

Tempe # 093
6460 S. McClintock Drive
Tempe, AZ 85283
Phone: 480-838-4142

Tucson (Crossroads) # 088
4766 East Grant Road
Tucson, AZ 85712
Phone: 520-323-4500

Tucson (Wilmot & Speedway)# 095
1101 N. Wilmot Rd. Suite #147
Tucson, AZ 85712
Trading Hours: 8 am- 9 pm
Phone: 520-733-1313

**Tucson (Campbell &
Limberlost) # 191**
4209 N. Campbell Ave.
Tucson, AZ 85719
Phone: 520-325-0069

Tucson - Oro Valley # 096
7912 N. Oracle
Oro Valley, AZ 85704
Phone: 520-797-4207

CALIFORNIA

Alameda # 109
2217 South Shore Center
Alameda, CA 94501
Phone: 510-769-5450

Aliso Viejo # 195
The Commons
26541 Aliso Creek Road
Aliso Viejo, CA 92656
Phone: 949-643-5531

Arroyo Grande # 117
955 Rancho Parkway
Arroyo Grande, CA 93420
Phone: 805-474-6114

Bakersfield # 014
8200-C 21 Stockdale Hwy.
Bakersfield, CA 93311
Phone: 661-837-8863

Berkeley #186
1885 University Ave.
Berkeley, CA 94703
Phone: 510-204-9074

Bixby Knolls # 116
4121 Atlantic Ave.
Bixby Knolls, CA 90807
Phone: 562-988-0695

Brea # 011
2500 E. Imperial Hwy. Suite 177
Brea, CA 92821
Phone 714-257-1180

Brentwood # 201
5451 Lone Tree Way
Brentwood, CA 94513
Phone: 925-516-3044

Burbank # 124
214 East Alameda
Burbank, CA 91502
Phone: 818-848-4299

Camarillo # 114
363 Carmen Drive
Camarillo, CA 93010
Phone: 805-388-1925

Campbell # 073
1875 Bascom Avenue
Campbell, CA 95008
Trading Hours: 8 am – 9 pm
Phone: 408-369-7823

Capitola # 064
3555 Clares Street #D
Capitola, CA 95010
Phone: 831-464-0115

Carlsbad # 220
2629 Gateway Road
Carlsbad, CA 92009
Phone: 760-603-8473

Castro Valley # 084
22224 Redwood Road
Castro Valley, CA 94546
Phone: 510-538-2738

Cathedral City # 118
67-720 East Palm Cyn.
Cathedral City, CA 92234
Phone: 760-202-0090

Cerritos # 104
12861 Towne Center Drive
Cerritos, CA 90703
Phone: 562-402-5148

Chatsworth # 184
10330 Mason Ave.
Chatsworth, CA 91311
Phone: 818-341-3010

Chico # 199
801 East Ave., Suite #110
Chico, CA 95926
Phone: 530-343-9920

Chino Hills # 216
13911 Peyton Dr.
Chino Hills, CA 91709
Phone: 909-627-1404

Chula Vista # 120
878 Eastlake Parkway, Suite 810
Chula Vista, CA 91914
Phone: 619-656-5370

Claremont # 214
475 W. Foothill Blvd.
Claremont, CA 91711
Phone: 909-625-8784

Clovis # 180
1077 N. Willow, Suite 101
Clovis, CA 93611
Phone: 559-325-3120

Concord (Oak Grove & Treat) # 083
785 Oak Grove Road
Concord, CA 94518
Phone: 925-521-1134

Concord (Airport) # 060
1150 Concord Ave.
Concord, CA 94520
Phone: 925-689-2990

Corona # 213
2790 Cabot Drive, Ste. 165
Corona, CA 92883
Phone: 951-603-0299

Costa Mesa # 035
640 W. 17th Street
Costa Mesa, CA 92627
Phone: 949-642-5134

Culver City # 036
9290 Culver Blvd.
Culver City, CA 90232
Phone: 310-202-1108

Daly City # 074
417 Westlake Center
Daly City, CA 94015
Phone: 650-755-3825

Danville # 065
85 Railroad Ave.
Danville, CA 94526
Phone: 925-838-5757

Eagle Rock # 055
1566 Colorado Blvd.
Eagle Rock, CA 90041
Phone: 323-257-6422

El Cerrito # 108
225 El Cerrito Plaza
El Cerrito, CA 94530
Phone: 510-524-7609

Elk Grove # 190
9670 Bruceville Road
Elk Grove, CA 95757
Phone: 916-686-9980

Emeryville # 072
5700 Christie Avenue
Emeryville, CA 94608
Phone: 510-658-8091

Encinitas # 025
115 N. El Camino Real, Suite A
Encinitas, CA 92024
Phone: 760-634-2114

Encino # 056
17640 Burbank Blvd.
Encino, CA 91316
Phone: 818-990-7751

Escondido # 105
1885 So. Centre City Pkwy.,
Unit "A"
Escondido, CA 92025
Phone: 760-233-4020

Fair Oaks # 071
5309 Sunrise Blvd.
Fair Oaks, CA 95628
Phone: 916-863-1744

Fairfield # 101
1350 Gateway Blvd., Suite A1-A7
Fairfield, CA 94533
Phone: 707-434-0144

Folsom # 172
850 East Bidwell
Folsom, CA 95630
Phone: 916-817-8820

Fremont # 077
39324 Argonaut Way
Fremont, CA 94538
Phone: 510-794-1386

Fresno # 008
5376 N. Blackstone
Fresno, CA 93710
Phone: 559-222-4348

Glendale # 053
130 N. Glendale Ave.
Glendale, CA 91206
Phone: 818-637-2990

Goleta # 110
5767 Calle Real
Goleta, CA 93117
Phone: 805-692-2234

Granada Hills # 044
11114 Balboa Blvd.
Granada Hills, CA 91344
Phone: 818-368-6461

Hollywood
1600 N. Vine Street
Los Angeles, CA 90028
Phone: 323-856-0689

Huntington Bch. # 047
18681-101 Main Street
Huntington Bch., CA 92648
Phone: 714-848-9640

Huntington Bch. # 241
21431 Brookhurst St.
Huntington Bch., CA 92646
Phone: 714-968-4070

Huntington Harbor # 244
Huntington Harbour Mall
16821 Algonquin St.
Huntington Bch., CA 92649
Phone: 714-846-7307

Irvine (Walnut Village Center) # 037
14443 Culver Drive
Irvine, CA 92604
Phone: 949-857-8108

Irvine (University Center) # 111
4225 Campus Dr.
Irvine, CA 92612
Phone: 949-509-6138

Irvine (Irvine & Sand Cyn) # 210
6222 Irvine Blvd.
Irvine, CA 92620
Phone: 949-551-6402

La Cañada # 042
475 Foothill Blvd.
La Canada, CA 91011
Phone: 818-790-6373

La Crescenta # 052
3433 Foothill Blvd.
LaCrescenta, CA 91214
Phone: 818-249-3693

La Quinta # 189
46-400 Washington Street
La Quinta, CA 92253
Phone: 760-777-1553

Lafayette # 115
3649 Mt. Diablo Blvd.
Lafayette, CA 94549
Phone: 925-299-9344

Laguna Hills # 039
24321 Avenue De La Carlota
Laguna Hills, CA 92653
Phone: 949-586-8453

Laguna Niguel # 103
32351 Street of the Golden
Lantern
Laguna Niguel, CA 92677
Phone: 949-493-8599

La Jolla # 020
8657 Villa LaJolla Drive #210
La Jolla, CA 92037
Phone: 858-546-8629

La Mesa # 024
5495 Grossmont Center Dr.
La Mesa, CA 91942
Phone: 619-466-0105

Larkspur # 235
2052 Redwood Hwy
Larkspur, CA 94921
Phone: 415-945-7955

Livermore # 208
1122-A East Stanley Blvd.
Livermore, CA 94550
Phone: 925-243-1947

Long Beach (PCH) # 043
6451 E. Pacific Coast Hwy.
Long Beach, CA 90803
Phone: 562-596-4388

Long Beach (Bellflower Blvd.) # 194
2222 Bellflower Blvd.
Long Beach, CA 90815
Phone: 562-596-2514

Los Altos # 127
2310 Homestead Rd.
Los Altos, CA 94024
Phone: 408-245-1917

Los Angeles (Silver Lake) # 017
2738 Hyperion Ave.
Los Angeles, CA 90027
Phone: 323-665-6774

Los Angeles # 031
263 S. La Brea
Los Angeles, CA 90036
Phone: 323-965-1989

Los Angeles (Sunset Strip) # 192
8000 Sunset Blvd.
Los Angeles, CA 90046
Phone: 323-822-7663

Los Gatos # 181
15466 Los Gatos Blvd.
Los Gatos, CA 95032
Phone 408-356-2324

Manhattan Beach # 034
1821 Manhattan Beach. Blvd.
Manhattan Bch., CA 90266
Phone: 310-372-1274

Manhattan Beach # 196
1800 Rosecrans Blvd.
Manhattan Beach, CA 90266
Phone: 310-725-9800

Menlo Park # 069
720 Menlo Avenue
Menlo Park, CA 94025
Phone: 650-323-2134

Millbrae # 170
765 Broadway
Millbrae, CA 94030
Phone: 650-259-9142

Mission Viejo # 126
25410 Marguerite Parkway
Mission Viejo, CA 92692
Phone: 949-581-5638

Modesto # 009
3250 Dale Road
Modesto, CA 95356
Phone: 209-491-0445

Monrovia # 112
604 W. Huntington Dr.
Monrovia, CA 91016
Phone: 626-358-8884

Monterey # 204
570 Munras Ave., Ste. 20
Monterey, CA 93940
Phone: 831-372-2010

Morgan Hill # 202
17035 Laurel Road
Morgan Hill, CA 95037
Phone: 408-778-6409

Mountain View # 081
590 Showers Dr.
Mountain View, CA 94040
Phone: 650-917-1013

Napa # 128
3654 Bel Aire Plaza
Napa, CA 94558
Phone: 707-256-0806

Newbury Park # 243
125 N. Reino Road
Newbury Park, CA
Phone: 805-375-1984

Newport Beach # 125
8086 East Coast Highway
Newport Beach, CA 92657
Phone: 949-494-7404

Novato # 198
7514 Redwood Blvd.
Novato, CA 94945
Phone: 415-898-9359

Oakland (Lakeshore) # 203
3250 Lakeshore Ave.
Oakland, CA 94610
Phone: 510-238-9076

Oakland (Rockridge) # 231
5727 College Ave.
Oakland, CA 94618
Phone: 510-923-9428

Oceanside # 22
2570 Vista Way
Oceanside, CA 92054
Phone: 760-433-9994

Orange # 046
2114 N. Tustin St.
Orange, CA 92865
Phone: 714-283-5697

Pacific Grove # 008
1170 Forest Avenue
Pacific Grove, CA 93950
Phone: 831-656-0180

Palm Desert # 003
44-250 Town Center Way,
Suite C6
Palm Desert, CA 92260
Phone: 760-340-2291

Palmdale # 185
39507 10th Street West
Palmdale, CA 93551
Phone: 661-947-2890

Palo Alto # 207
855 El Camino Real
Palo Alto, CA 94301
Phone: 650-327-7018

Pasadena (S. Lake Ave.) # 179
345 South Lake Ave.
Pasadena, CA 91101
Phone: 626-395-9553

Pasadena (S. Arroyo Pkwy.) # 051
610 S. Arroyo Parkway
Pasadena, CA 91105
Phone: 626-568-9254

Pasadena (Hastings Ranch) # 171
467 Rosemead Blvd.
Pasadena, CA 91107
Phone: 626-351-3399

Petaluma # 107
169 North McDowell Blvd.
Petaluma, CA 94954
Phone: 707-769-2782

Pinole # 230
2742 Pinole Valley Rd.
Pinole, CA 94564
Phone: 510-222-3501

Pleasanton # 066
4040 Pimlico #150
Pleasanton, CA 94588
Phone: 925-225-3600

Rancho Cucamonga # 217
6401 Haven Ave.
Rancho Cucamonga, CA 91737
Phone: 909-476-1410

Rancho Palos Verdes # 057
28901 S. Western Ave. #243
Rancho Palos Verdes, CA 90275
Phone: 310-832-1241

Rancho Palos Verdes # 233
31176 Hawthorne Blvd.
Rancho Palos Verdes, CA 90275
Phone: 310-544-1727

Rancho Santa Margarita # 027
30652 Santa Margarita Pkwy.
Suite F102
Rcho Santa Margarita, CA 92688
Phone: 949-888-3640

Redding # 219
845 Browning St.
Redding, CA 96003
Phone: 530-223-4875

Redlands # 099
552 Orange Street Plaza
Redlands, CA 92374
Phone: 909-798-3888

Redondo Beach # 038
1761 S. Elena Avenue
Redondo Bch., CA 90277
Phone: 310-316-1745

Riverside # 15
6225 Riverside Plaza
Riverside, CA 92506
Phone: 951-682-4684

Roseville # 80
1117 Roseville Square
Roseville, CA 95678
Phone: 916-784-9084

Sacramento (Folsom Blvd.) # 175
5000 Folsom Blvd.
Sacramento, CA 95819
Phone: 916-456-1853

**Sacramento
(Fulton & Marconi) # 070**
2625 Marconi Avenue
Sacramento, CA 95821
Phone: 916-481-8797

San Carlos # 174
1482 El Camino Real
San Carlos, CA 94070
Phone: 650-594-2138

San Clemente # 016
638 Camino DeLosMares,
Sp.#115-G
San Clemente, CA 92673
Phone: 949-240-9996

San Diego (Hillcrest) # 026
1090 University Ste. G100-107
San Diego, CA 92103
Phone: 619-296-3122

San Diego (Point Loma) # 188
2401 Truxtun Rd., Ste. 300
San Diego, CA 92106
Phone: 619-758-9272

San Diego (Pacific Beach) # 021
1211 Garnet Avenue
San Diego, CA 92109
Phone: 858-272-7235

**San Diego
(Carmel Mtn. Ranch) # 023**
11955 Carmel Mtn. Rd. #702
San Diego, CA 92128
Phone: 858-673-0526

San Diego (Scripps Ranch) # 221
9850 Hibert Street
San Diego, CA 92131
Phone: 858-549-9185

San Dimas # 028
856 Arrow Hwy. "C" Target
Center
San Dimas, CA 91773
Phone: 909-305-4757

San Francisco (9th Street) # 078
555 9th Street
San Francisco, CA 94103
Phone: 415-863-1292

San Francisco (Masonic Ave.) # 100
3 Masonic Avenue
San Francisco, CA 94118
Phone: 415-346-9964

San Francisco (North Beach) # 019
401 Bay Street
San Francisco, CA 94133
Phone: 415-351-1013

San Francisco (Stonestown) # 236
265 Winston Dr.
San Francisco, CA 94132
Phone: 415-665-1835

San Gabriel # 032
7260 N. Rosemead Blvd.
San Gabriel, CA 91775
Phone: 626-285-5862

San Jose (Bollinger) # 232
7250 Bollinger Rd.
San Jose, CA 95129
Phone: 408-873-7384

San Jose (Coleman Ave.) # 212
635 Coleman Ave.
San Jose, CA 95110
Phone: 408-298-9731

San Jose (Old Almaden) # 063
5353 Almaden Expressway #J-38
San Jose, CA 95118
Phone: 408-927-9091

San Jose (Westgate West) # 062
5269 Prospect
San Jose, CA 95129
Phone: 408-446-5055

San Luis Obispo # 041
3977 Higuera Street
San Luis Obispo, CA 93401
Phone: 805-783-2780

San Mateo (Grant Street) # 067
1820-22 S. Grant Street
San Mateo, CA 94402
Phone: 650-570-6140

San Mateo (Hillsdale) # 245
45 W Hillsdale Blvd
San Mateo, CA 94403
Phone: 650-286-1509

San Rafael # 061
337 Third Street
San Rafael, CA 94901
Phone: 415-454-9530

Santa Ana # 113
3329 South Bristol Street
Santa Ana, CA 92704
Phone: 714-424-9304

Santa Barbara (S. Milpas St.) # 059
29 S. Milpas Street
Santa Barbara, CA 93103
Phone: 805-564-7878

Santa Barbara (De La Vina) # 183
3025 De La Vina
Santa Barbara, CA 93105
Phone: 805-563-7383

Santa Cruz # 193
700 Front Street
Santa Cruz, CA 95060
Phone: 831-425-0140

Santa Maria # 239
1303 S. Bradley Road
Santa Maria, CA 93454
Phone: 805-925-1657

Santa Monica # 006
3212 Pico Blvd.
Santa Monica, CA 90405
Phone: 310-581-0253

Santa Rosa (Cleveland Ave.) # 075
3225 Cleveland Avenue
Santa Rosa, CA 95403
Phone: 707-525-1406

Santa Rosa (Santa Rosa Ave.) # 178
2100 Santa Rosa Ave.
Santa Rosa, CA 95407
Phone: 707-535-0788

Sherman Oaks # 049
14119 Riverside Drive
Sherman Oaks, CA 91423
Phone: 818-789-2771

Simi Valley # 030
2975-A Cochran St.
Simi Valley, CA 93065
Phone: 805-520-3135

South Pasadena # 018
613 Mission Street
South Pasadena, CA 91030
Phone: 626-441-6263

South San Francisco # 187
301 McLellan Dr.
So. San Francisco, CA 94080
Phone: 650-583-6401

Stockton # 076
6535 Pacific Avenue
Stockton, CA 95207
Phone: 209-951-7597

Studio City # 122
11976 Ventura Blvd.
Studio City, CA 91604
Phone: 818-509-0168

Sunnyvale # 068
727 Sunnyvale/Saratoga Rd.
Sunnyvale, CA 94087
Phone: 408-481-9082

Temecula # 102
40665 Winchester Rd., Bldg. B,
Ste. 4-6
Temecula, CA 92591
Phone: 951-296-9964

Templeton # 211
1111 Rossi Road
Templeton, CA 93465
Phone: 805-434-9562

Thousand Oaks # 196
451 Avenida De Los Arboles
Thousand Oaks, CA 91360
Phone: 805-492-7107

Toluca Lake # 054
10130 Riverside Drive
Toluca Lake, CA 91602
Phone: 818-762-2787

Torrance (Hawthorne Blvd.) # 121
19720 Hawthorne Blvd.
Torrance, CA 90503
Phone: 310-793-8585

Torrance (Rolling Hills Plaza) # 029
2545 Pacific Coast Highway
Torrance, CA 90505
Phone: 310-326-9520

Tustin # 197
12932 Newport Avenue
Tustin, CA 92780
Phone: 714-669-3752

Upland # 010
333 So. Mountain Avenue
Upland, CA 91786
Phone: 909-946-4799

Valencia # 013
26517 Bouquet Canyon Rd
Santa Clarita, CA 91350
Phone: 661-263-3796

Ventura # 045
1795 S. Victoria Avenue
Ventura, CA 93003
Phone: 805-650-9977

Walnut Creek # 123
1372 So. California Blvd.
Walnut Creek, CA 94596
Phone: 925-945-1674

West Hills # 050
6751 Fallbrook Ave.
West Hills, CA 91307
Phone: 818-347-2591

West Hollywood # 040
7304 Santa Monica Blvd.
West Hollywood, CA 90046
Phone: 323-851-9772

West Hollywood # 173
8611 Santa Monica Blvd.
West Hollywood, CA 90069
Phone 310-657-0152

**West Los Angeles
(National Blvd.) # 007**
10850 National Blvd.
West Los Angeles, CA 90064
Phone: 310-470-1917

**West Los Angeles
(S. Sepulveda Blvd.) # 119**
3456 S. Sepulveda Blvd.
West Los Angeles, CA 90034
Phone: 310-836-2458

West Los Angeles (Olympic) # 215
11755 W. Olympic Blvd.
West Los Angeles, CA 90064
Phone: 310-477-5949

Westchester # 033
8645 S. Sepulveda
Westchester, CA 90045
Phone: 310-338-9238

Westlake Village # 058
3835 E. Thousand Oaks Blvd.
Westlake Village, CA 91362
Phone: 805-494-5040

Westwood # 234
1000 Glendon Avenue
Los Angeles, CA 90024
Phone: 310-824-1495

Whittier # 048
15025 E. Whittier Blvd.
Whittier, CA 90603
Phone: 562-698-1642

Woodland Hills # 209
21054 Clarendon St.
Woodland Hills, CA 91364
Phone: 818-712-9475

Yorba Linda # 176
19655 Yorba Linda Blvd.
Yorba Linda, CA 92886
Phone: 714-970-0116

CONNECTICUT

Danbury # 525
113 Mill Plain Rd.
Danbury, CT 06811
Phone: 203-739-0098
Alcohol: Beer Only

Darien # 522
436 Boston Post Rd.
Darien, CT 06820
Phone: 203-656-1414
Alcohol: Beer Only

Fairfield # 523
2258 Black Rock Turnpike
Fairfield, CT 06825
Phone: 203-330-8301
Alcohol: Beer Only

Orange # 524
560 Boston Post Road
Orange, CT 06477
Phone: 203-795-5505
Alcohol: Beer Only

West Hartford # 526
1489 New Britain Ave.
West Hartford, CT 06110
Phone: 860-561-4771
Alcohol: Beer Only

Westport # 521
400 Post Road East
Westport, CT 06880
Phone: 203-226-8966
Alcohol: Beer Only

DELAWARE

Wilmington* # 536
5605 Concord Pike
Wilmington, DE 19803
Phone: 302-478-8494

DISTRICT OF COLUMBIA

Washington # 653
1101 25th Street NW
Washington, DC 20037
Phone: 202-296-1921

GEORGIA

Atlanta (Buckhead) # 735
3183 Peachtree Rd NE
Atlanta, GA 30305
Phone: 404-842-0907

Atlanta (Midtown) # 730
931 Monroe Dr., NE
Atlanta, GA 30308
Phone: 404-815-9210

Marietta # 732
4250 Roswell Road
Marietta, GA 30062
Phone: 678-560-3585

Norcross # 734
5185 Peachtree Parkway, Bld.
1200
Norcross, GA 30092
Phone: 678-966-9236

Roswell # 733
635 W. Crossville Road
Roswell, GA 30075
Phone: 770-645-8505

Sandy Springs # 731
6277 Roswell Road NE
Sandy Springs, GA 30328
Phone: 404-236-2414

ILLINOIS

Algonquin # 699
1800 South Randall Road
Algonquin, IL 60102
Phone: 847-854-4886

Arlington Heights # 687
17 W. Rand Road
Arlington Heights, IL 60004
Phone: 847-506-0752

Batavia # 689
1942 West Fabyan Parkway #222
Batavia, IL 60510
Phone: 630-879-3234

Chicago (River North) # 696
44 E. Ontario St.
Chicago, IL 60611
Phone: 312-951-6369

Chicago (Lincoln & Grace) # 688
3745 North Lincoln Avenue
Chicago, IL 60613
Phone: 773-248-4920

Chicago (Lincoln Park) # 691
1840 North Clybourn Avenue
#200
Chicago, IL 60614
Phone: 312-274-9733

Downers Grove # 683
122 Ogden Ave.
Downers Grove, IL 60515
Phone: 630-241-1662

Glen Ellyn # 680
680 Roosevelt Rd.
Glen Ellyn, IL 60137
Phone: 630-858-5077

Glenview # 681
1407 Waukegan Road
Glenview, IL 60025
Phone: 847-657-7821

La Grange # 685
25 North La Grange Road
La Grange, IL 60525
Phone: 708-579-0838

Lake Zurich # 684
735 W. Route 22**
Lake Zurich, IL 60047
Phone: 847-550-7827
[**For accurate driving
directions using GPS, please
use 735 W Main Street]

Naperville # 690
44 West Gartner Road
Naperville, IL 60540
Phone: 630-355-4389

Northbrook # 682
127 Skokie Blvd.
Northbrook, IL 60062
Phone: 847-498-9076

Oak Park # 697
483 N. Harlem Ave.
Oak Park, IL 60301
Phone: 708-386-1169

Orland Park # 686
14924 S. La Grange Road
Orland Park, IL 60462
Phone: 708-349-9021

Park Ridge # 698
190 North Northwest Highway
Park Ridge, IL 60068
Phone: 847-292-1108

* Store does not carry alcohol

INDIANA

Indianapolis (Castleton) # 671
5473 East 82nd Street
Indianapolis, IN 46250
Phone: 317-595-8950

Indianapolis (West 86th) # 670
2902 West 86th Street
Indianapolis, IN 46268
Phone: 317-337-1880

MARYLAND

Annapolis* # 650
160 F Jennifer Road
Annapolis, MD 21401
Phone: 410-573-0505

Bethesda* # 645
6831 Wisconsin Avenue
Bethesda, MD 20815
Phone: 301-907-0982

Columbia* # 658
6610 Marie Curie Dr. (Int. of 175 & 108)
Elkridge, MD 21075
Phone: 410-953-8139

Gaithersburg* # 648
18270 Contour Rd.
Gaithersburg, MD 20877
Trading Hours: 8 am – 9 pm
Phone: 301-947-5953

Pikesville* # 655
1809 Reisterstown Road, Suite #121
Pikesville, MD 21208
Phone: 410-484-8373

Rockville* # 642
12268-H Rockville Pike
Rockville, MD 20852
Phone: 301-468-6656

Silver Spring* # 652
10741 Columbia Pike
Silver Spring, MD 20901
Phone: 301-681-1675

Towson* # 649
1 E. Joppa Rd.
Towson, MD 21286
Phone: 410-296-9851

MASSACHUSETTS

Acton* # 511
145 Great Road
Acton, MA 01720
Phone: 978-266-8908

Arlington* # 505
1427 Massachusetts Ave.
Arlington, MA 02476
Phone: 781-646-9138

Boston* # 510
899 Boylston Street
Boston, MA 02115
Phone: 617-262-6505

Brookline* # 501
1317 Beacon Street
Brookline, MA 02446
Phone: 617-278-9997

Burlington* # 515
51 Middlesex Turnpike
Burlington, MA 01803
Phone: 781-273-2310

Cambridge
748 Memorial Drive
Cambridge, MA 02139
Phone: 617-491-8582

Cambridge (Fresh Pond)* # 517
211 Alewife Brook Pkwy
Cambridge, MA 02138
Phone: 617-498-3201

Framingham # 503
659 Worcester Road
Framingham, MA 01701
Phone: 508-935-2931

Hadley* # 512
375 Russell Street
Hadley, MA 01035
Phone: 413-587-3260

Hanover* # 513
1775 Washington Street
Hanover, MA 02339
Phone: 781-826-5389

Hyannis* # 514
Christmas Tree Promenade
655 Route 132, Unit 4-A
Hyannis, MA 02601
Phone: 508-790-3008

Needham Hts* 504
958 Highland Avenue
Needham Hts, MA 02494
Phone: 781-449-6993

Peabody* # 516
300 Andover Street, Suite 15
Peabody, MA 01960
Phone: 978-977-5316

Saugus* # 506
358 Broadway, Unit B
(Shops @ Saugus, Rte. 1)
Saugus, MA 01906
Phone: 781-231-0369

Shrewsbury* # 508
77 Boston Turnpike
Shrewsbury, MA 01545
Phone: 508-755-9560

Tyngsboro* # 507
440 Middlesex Road
Tyngsboro, MA 01879
Phone: 978-649-2726

West Newton* # 509
1121 Washington St.
West Newton, MA 02465
Phone: 617-244-1620

MICHIGAN

Ann Arbor # 678
2398 East Stadium Blvd.
Ann Arbor, MI 48104
Phone: 734-975-2455

Farmington Hills # 675
31221 West 14 Mile Road
Farmington Hills, MI 48334
Phone: 248-737-4609

Grosse Pointe # 665
17028 Kercheval Ave.
Grosse Pointe, MI 48230
Phone: 313-640-7794

Northville # 667
20490 Haggerty Road
Northville, MI 48167
Phone: 734-464-3675

Rochester Hills # 668
3044 Walton Blvd.
Rochester Hills, MI 48309
Phone: 248-375-2190

Royal Oak # 674
27880 Woodward Ave.
Royal Oak, MI 48067
Phone: 248-582-9002

MINNESOTA

Maple Grove # 713
12105 Elm Creek Blvd. N.
Maple Grove, MN 55369
Phone: 763-315-1739

Minnetonka # 714
11220 Wayzata Blvd
Minnetonka, MN 55305
Phone: 952-417-9080

St. Louis Park # 710
4500 Excelsior Blvd.
St. Louis Park, MN 55416
Phone: 952-285-1053

St. Paul # 716
484 Lexington Parkway S.
St. Paul, MN 55116
Phone: 651-698-3119

Woodbury # 715
8960 Hudson Road
Woodbury, MN 55125
Phone: 651-735-0269

MISSOURI

Brentwood # 792
48 Brentwood Promenade Court
Brentwood, MO 63144
Phone: 314-963-0253

Chesterfield # 693
1679 Clarkson Road
Chesterfield, MO 63017
Phone: 636-536-7846

Creve Coeur # 694
11505 Olive Blvd.
Creve Coeur, MO 63141
Phone: 314-569-0427

Des Peres # 695
13343 Manchester Rd.
Des Peres, MO 63131
Phone: 314-984-5051

NEBRASKA

Omaha # 714 - Coming Soon!
10305 Pacific St.
Omaha, NE 68114
Phone: TBD

NEVADA

Anthem # 280
10345 South Eastern Ave.
Henderson, NV 89052
Phone: 702-407-8673

Carson City # 281
3790 US Highway 395 S,
Suite 401
Carson City, NV 89705
Phone: 775-267-2486

Henderson # 097
2716 North Green Valley
Parkway
Henderson, NV 89014
Phone: 702-433-6773

Las Vegas (Decatur Blvd.) # 098
2101 S. Decatur Blvd., Suite 25
Las Vegas, NV 89102
Phone: 702-367-0227

Store does not carry alcohol

Las Vegas (Summerlin) # 086
7575 West Washington, Suite 117
Las Vegas, NV 89128
Phone: 702-242-8240

Reno # 082
5035 S. McCarran Blvd.
Reno, NV 89502
Phone: 775-826-1621

NEW JERSEY

Edgewater* # 606
715 River Road
Edgewater, NJ 07020
Phone: 201-945-5932

Florham Park* # 604
186 Columbia Turnpike
Florham Park, NJ 07932
Phone: 973-514-1511

Marlton* # 631
300 P Route 73 South
Marlton, NJ 08053
Phone: 856-988-3323

Millburn* # 609
187 Millburn Ave.
Millburn, NJ 07041
Phone: 973-218-0912

Paramus* # 605
404 Rt. 17 North
Paramus, NJ 07652
Phone: 201-265-9624

Princeton # 607
3528 US 1 (Brunswick Pike)
Princeton, NJ 08540
Phone: 609-897-0581

Wayne* # 632
1172 Hamburg Turnpike
Wayne, NJ 07470
Phone: 973-692-0050

Westfield # 601
155 Elm St.
Westfield, NJ 07090
Phone: 908-301-0910

Westwood* # 602
20 Irvington Street
Westwood, NJ 07675
Phone: 201-263-0134

NEW MEXICO

Albuquerque # 166
8928 Holly Ave. NE
Albuquerque, NM 87122
Phone: 505-796-0311

Albuquerque (Uptown) # 167
2200 Uptown Loop NE
Albuquerque, NM 87110
Phone: 505-883-3662

Santa Fe # 165
530 W. Cordova Road
Santa Fe, NM 87505
Phone: 505-995-8145

NEW YORK

**72nd & Broadway # 542 -
Coming Soon!**
2075 Broadway
New York, NY 10023
Phone: TBD

Brooklyn # 558
130 Court St
Brooklyn, NY 11201
Phone: 718-246-8460
Alcohol: Beer Only

Chelsea # 543
675 6th Ave
New York, NY 10010
Phone: 212-255-2106
Alcohol: Beer Only

Commack* # 551
5010 Jericho Turnpike
Commack, NY 11725
Phone: 631-493-9210

Hartsdale* # 533
215 North Central Avenue
Hartsdale, NY 10530
Phone: 914-997-1960

Hewlett* # 554
1280 West Broadway
Hewlett, NY 11557
Phone: 516-569-7191

Lake Grove* # 556
137 Alexander Ave.
Lake Grove, NY 11755
Phone: 631-863-2477

Larchmont* # 532
1260 Boston Post Road
Larchmont, NY 10538
Phone: 914-833-9110

Merrick* # 553
1714 Merrick Road
Merrick, NY 11566
Phone: 516-771-1012

**New York (Union Square
Grocery) # 540**
142 E. 14th St.
New York, NY 10003
Phone: 212-529-4612
Alcohol: Beer Only

**New York (Union Square
Wine) # 541**
138 E. 14th St.
New York, NY 10003
Phone: 212-529-6326
Alcohol: Wine Only

Oceanside* # 552
3418 Long Beach Rd.
Oceanside, NY 11572
Phone: 516-536-9163

Plainview* # 555
425 S. Oyster Bay Rd.
Plainview, NY 11803
Phone: 516-933-6900

Queens* # 557
90-30 Metropolitan Ave.
Queens, NY 11374
Phone: 718-275-1791

Scarsdale* # 531
727 White Plains Rd.
Scarsdale, NY 10583
Phone: 914-472-2988

NORTH CAROLINA

Cary # 741
1393 Kildaire Farms Rd.
Cary, NC 27511
Phone: 919-465-5984

Chapel Hill # 745
1800 E. Franklin St.
Chapel Hill, NC 27514
Phone: 919-918-7871

Charlotte (Midtown) # 744
1133 Metropolitan Ave., Ste. 100
Charlotte, NC 28204
Phone: 704-334-0737

Charlotte (North) # 743
1820 East Arbors Dr.** (corner
of W. Mallard Creek Church Rd.
& Senator Royall Dr.)
Charlotte, NC 28262
Phone: 704-688-9578
[**For accurate driving direc-
tions on the web, please use 1820
W. Mallard Creek Church Rd.]

Charlotte (South) # 742
6418 Rea Rd.
Charlotte, NC 28277
Phone: 704-543-5249

Raleigh # 746
3000 Wake Forest Rd.
Raleigh, NC 27609
Phone: 919-981-7422

OHIO

Cincinnati # 669
7788 Montgomery Road
Cincinnati, OH 45236
Phone: 513-984-3452

Columbus # 679
3888 Townsfair Way
Columbus, OH 43219
Phone: 614-473-0794

Dublin # 672
6355 Sawmill Road
Dublin, OH 43017
Phone: 614-793-8505

Kettering # 673
328 East Stroop Road
Kettering, OH 45429
Phone: 937-294-5411

Westlake # 677
175 Market Street
Westlake, OH 44145
Phone: 440-250-1592

Woodmere # 676
28809 Chagrin Blvd.
Woodmere, OH 44122
Phone: 216-360-9320

OREGON

Beaverton # 141
11753 S. W. Beaverton Hillsdale
Hwy.
Beaverton, OR 97005
Phone: 503-626-3794

Bend # 150
63455 North Highway 97, Ste. 4
Bend, OR 97701
Phone: 541-312-4198

Clackamas # 152
9345 SE 82nd Ave (across from
Home Depot)
Happy Valley, OR 97086
Phone: 503-771-6300

Corvallis # 154
1550 NW 9th Street
Corvallis, OR 97330
Phone: 541-753-0048

Eugene # 145
85 Oakway Center
Eugene, OR 97401
Phone: 541-485-1744

Hillsboro # 149
2285 NW 185th Ave.
Hillsboro, OR 97124
Phone: 503-645-8321

* Store does not carry alcohol

Lake Oswego # 142
15391 S. W. Bangy Rd.
Lake Oswego, OR 97035
Phone: 503-639-3238

Portland (SE) # 143
4715 S. E. 39th Avenue
Portland, OR 97202
Phone: 503-777-1601

Portland (NW) # 146
2122 N.W. Glisan
Portland, OR 97210
Phone: 971-544-0788

Portland (Hollywood) # 144
4121 N.E. Halsey St.
Portland, OR 97213
Phone: 503-284-1694

PENNSYLVANIA

Ardmore* # 635
112 Coulter Avenue
Ardmore, PA 19003
Phone: 610-658-0645

Jenkintown* # 633
933 Old York Road
Jenkintown, PA 19046
Phone: 215-885-524

Media* # 637
12 East State Street
Media, PA 19063
Phone: 610-891-2752

North Wales* # 639
1430 Bethlehem Pike (corner SR
309 & SR 63)
North Wales, PA 19454
Phone: 215-646-5870

Philadelphia* # 634
2121 Market Street
Philadelphia, PA 19103
Phone: 215-569-9282

Pittsburgh* # 638
6343 Penn Ave.
Pittsburgh, PA 15206
Trading Hours: 8 am – 9 pm
Phone: 412-363-5748

Wayne* # 632
171 East Swedesford Rd.
Wayne, PA 19087
Phone: 610-225-0925

RHODE ISLAND

Warwick* # 518
1000 Bald Hill Rd
Warwick, RI 02886
Phone: 401-821-5368

TENNESSEE

Nashville # 664
3909 Hillsboro Pike
Nashville, TN 37215
Phone: 615-297-6560
Alcohol: Beer Only

VIRGINIA

Alexandria # 647
612 N. Saint Asaph Street
Alexandria, VA 22314
Phone: 703-548-0611

Bailey's Crossroads # 644
5847 Leesburg Pike
Bailey's Crossroads, VA 22041
Phone: 703-379-5883

Centreville # 654
14100 Lee Highway
Centreville, VA 20120
Phone: 703-815-0697

Fairfax # 643
9464 Main Street
Fairfax, VA 22031
Phone: 703-764-8550

Falls Church # 641
7514 Leesburg Turnpike
Falls Church, VA 22043
Phone: 703-288-0566

Newport News # 656
12551 Jefferson Ave., Suite #179
Newport News, VA 23602
Phone: 757-890-0235

Reston # 646
11958 Killingsworth Ave.
Reston, VA 20194
Phone: 703-689-0865

Richmond (Short Pump) # 659
11331 W Broad St, Ste 161
Glen Allen, VA 23060
Phone: 804-360-4098

Springfield # 651
6394 Springfield Plaza
Springfield, VA 22150
Phone: 703-569-9301

Virginia Beach # 660
503 Hilltop Plaza
Virginia Beach, VA 23454
Phone: 757-422-4840

Williamsburg # 657
5000 Settlers Market Blvd
(corner of Monticello and
Settlers Market)**
Williamsburg, VA 23188
Phone: 757-259-2135
[**For accurate driving
directions on the web, please
use 5224 Monticello Ave.]

WASHINGTON

Ballard # 147
4609 14th Avenue NW
Seattle, WA 98107
Phone: 206-783-0498

Bellevue # 131
15400 N. E. 20th Street
Bellevue, WA 98007
Phone: 425-643-6885

Bellingham # 151
2410 James Street
Bellingham, WA 98225
Phone: 360-734-5166

Burien # 133
15868 1st. Avenue South
Burien, WA 98148
Phone: 206-901-9339

Everett # 139
811 S.E. Everett Mall Way
Everett, WA 98208
Phone: 425-513-2210

Federal Way # 134
1758 S. 320th Street
Federal Way, WA 98003
Phone: 253-529-9242

Issaquah # 138
1495 11th Ave. N.W.
Issaquah, WA 98027
Phone: 425-837-8088

Kirkland # 132
12632 120th Avenue N. E.
Kirkland, WA 98034
Phone: 425-823-1685

Lynnwood # 129
19500 Highway 99, Suite 100
Lynnwood, WA 98036
Phone: 425-744-1346

.Olympia # 156
Olympia West Center
1530 Black Lake Blvd.
Olympia, WA 98502
Phone: 360-352-7440

Redmond # 140
15932 Redmond Way
Redmond, WA 98052
Phone: 425-883-1624

Seattle (U. District) # 137
4555 Roosevelt Way NE
Seattle, WA 98105
Phone: 206-547-6299

Seattle (Queen Anne Hill) # 135
112 West Galer St.
Seattle, WA 98119
Phone: 206-378-5536

Seattle (Capitol Hill) # 130
1700 Madison St.
Seattle, WA 98122
Phone: 206-322-7268

University Place # 148
3800 Bridgeport Way West
University Place, WA 98466
Phone: 253-460-2672

Vancouver # 136
305 SE Chkalov Drive #B1
Vancouver, WA 98683
Phone: 360-883-9000

WISCONSIN

Glendale # 711
5600 North Port Washington
Road
Glendale, WI 53217
Phone: 414-962-3382

Madison # 712
1810 Monroe Street
Madison, WI 53711
Phone: 608-257-1916

* Store does not carry alcohol

Although we aim to ensure that the store location information contained here is correct, we will not be responsible for any errors or omissions.